A PARISIAN BISTRO

— La Fontaine de Mars in 50 recipes —

Recipes **LA FONTAINE DE MARS**
Texts **CÉCILE MASLAKIAN**

Photography **DELPHINE CONSTANTINI**
Set dressing **NATACHA ARNOULT**

Foreword **ROBERT DE NIRO**

ABRAMS / NEW YORK

*« Through the years, I've spent a lot of time in Paris, but I never knew about
La Fontaine de Mars until the hotel I was staying at recommended it. I'm glad they
did! It's always a pleasure to come back to Paris and to eat there. The bistro is
a quintessential Parisian establishment — the Paris that, as an American,
I envision and hope to experience. When one thinks about Paris, La Fontaine de
Mars is what one imagines. Great food, great wine! It never disappoints! »*

—— Robert De Niro

CONTENTS

1 —— LIFTING THE CURTAIN
ON A UNIQUE PLACE

2 —— REVEALING THE SECRETS
BEHIND THE SCENES

LIFTING THE CURTAIN
on a unique place

entrée

TIREZ

W hen the red velvet curtain covering the door of La Fontaine de Mars is drawn aside, it's a whole other world that's revealed. As soon as you cross the threshold, it's as though you've been transported to another age. The bustle of the Parisian street seems suddenly a long way off. Indeed, the traditional decor preserves the fantasy of a bygone Paris that's both timeless and reassuring. Here, nothing changes. It doesn't take much imagination to find yourself in a movie from the 1940s, listening to Arletty ordering the bistro's legendary homemade cassoulet in her typically sassy way, or in the latest offering from Woody Allen celebrating the Paris he loves so dearly. Each element of the interior reflects an ever-present past. The red checkered tablecloths are identical to those that dressed the tables before the War; the patterned floor tiles, the Thonet chairs, the red leather banquettes, the plates, the beaded lamps—nothing seems to have changed since the beginning of the last century. And yet.

Nestled in the shadow of the neighboring Eiffel Tower on the square facing the eponymous fountain, the restaurant is almost the same age as the venerable "Iron Lady". Opened in 1908, La Fontaine de Mars was, in its early youth, a modest bar that echoed with the voices of soldiers from the nearby military academy and hospital. It also sold bags of coal, as was common at the time.

The 1930s heralded a new era. In 1932, the bar was bought by a couple from Quercy, the Maranges, who turned it into a bistro, which became a good place to come and enjoy the traditional homecooked cuisine of the south-west of France. While Madame Marange was in the kitchen—duck confit and cassoulet were key dishes on the menu even back then—her husband looked after the customers in the dining room. Legend has it that it was at La Fontaine de Mars that Cahors wine was served for the first time in Paris.

Under the Maranges, La Fontaine de Mars found its own unique style, adopting the colors of a local bistro that would shine in the firmament of Parisian brasseries a few decades later. And although the recipes may have changed somewhat, the spirit of the place remains.

THE RED CHECKERED TABLECLOTHS
ARE IDENTICAL TO THOSE THAT DRESSED
THE TABLES BEFORE THE WAR;
THE PATTERNED FLOOR TILES, THE THONET
CHAIRS, THE RED LEATHER BANQUETTES,
THE PLATES, THE BEADED LAMPS—NOTHING
SEEMS TO HAVE CHANGED SINCE THE
BEGINNING OF THE LAST CENTURY. AND YET.

POACHED EGGS
IN RED WINE SAUCE

SERVES 6

PREP: 20 MINUTES
COOK: 25 MINUTES

Ingredients

2 cups (500 ml) Madiran red wine
1 cup (200 g) finely chopped shallots
1 bouquet garni
2 cups (500 ml) veal bouillon
Pinch of superfine sugar
1 teaspoon wine vinegar
3 ½ oz. (100 g) unsmoked slab bacon
4 teaspoons (½ oz./20 g) butter
12 eggs
Salt and pepper

Preheat the oven to 320°F (160°C).

In a small saucepan, reduce the red wine with half the shallots and the bouquet garni until just a thin film of wine is left in the bottom of the pan. Add the veal bouillon and simmer until the mixture coats the spoon. Season with salt and pepper. Stir in the sugar and vinegar, then strain the sauce through a fine mesh sieve. Keep it warm.

Dice the bacon, then blanch: put the diced bacon in a pan of cold water and heat until the water reaches boiling point. Drain the bacon and lightly brown in a skillet. Drain on paper towels and set aside.

In another skillet, gently fry the remaining shallots in the butter until soft. Set aside.

Put the wine sauce, bacon, and shallots in a saucepan and bring to a simmer.

Pour two ladles of hot wine sauce into each of six ovenproof ramekins and gently break two eggs on top. Cook for 6 minutes in the oven.

Serve immediately with slices of toast.

Enjoy with a Madiran "Bouscassé Vieilles Vignes" 2007 by Alain Brumont.

In 1963, the restaurant was sold to Monsieur and Madame Launay who, despite coming from Normandy and the Sologne (north and north-central France respectively), chose to continue the restaurant's southwestern culinary tradition. They made no notable changes to either the menu or the dining room. Indeed, the only indication that time had passed was the red of the tablecloths, which had faded with use. The bistro's regulars had grown older, too—or had changed. Manual workers continued to frequent the little bistro to enjoy its simple meals, but they were now joined by students from the neighborhood. The clientele also regularly included families, and it was not uncommon on Saturdays to hear a happy hubbub from the room on the first floor, where families would often come to celebrate first communions and the like. On weekdays, the occasional heckling of big civic lunches was certainly no less noisy, but when the hearty dishes arrived at the table, everyone managed to agree.

Toward the end of the War, Parisian bistros like La Fontaine de Mars were favored by the GIs who had come to liberate Paris. Some joyfully celebrated V-E Day here, which is something to reminisce about. Sometime earlier, in a more somber atmosphere, General de Gaulle's disciples had dined here in private to contrive the plans that would lead France to victory. Fortunately, no one knew about this until a long time afterward.

Once the war had ended and the American troops had returned home, the bistro became a base for the families of American soldiers who had come to France to visit the Normandy cemeteries where their loved ones were buried. Their pilgrimage naturally ended on Rue Saint-Dominique, with a hareng pomme à l'huile or a hearty blanquette.

The restaurant was also favored by American journalists: Patricia Wells, of the International Herald Tribune, was a regular diner.

MANUAL WORKERS CONTINUED TO FREQUENT THE LITTLE BISTRO TO ENJOY ITS SIMPLE MEALS, BUT THEY WERE NOW JOINED BY STUDENTS FROM THE NEIGHBORHOOD. THE CLIENTELE ALSO REGULARLY INCLUDED FAMILIES, AND IT WAS NOT UNCOMMON ON SATURDAYS TO HEAR A HAPPY HUBBUB FROM THE ROOM ON THE FIRST FLOOR, WHERE FAMILIES WOULD OFTEN COME TO CELEBRATE FIRST COMMUNIONS AND THE LIKE.

REAL EGG MAYO
WITH VEGETABLE MACÉDOINE

SERVES 6

PREP: 15 MINUTES
COOK: 30 MINUTES

Ingredients

9 eggs

FOR THE MAYONNAISE:
1 egg yolk beaten with 1 teaspoon water
½ tablespoon strong Dijon mustard
½ teaspoon wine vinegar
1 scant cup (200 ml) grapeseed oil
Salt and freshly ground pepper

FOR THE VEGETABLES:
5 oz. (150 g) carrots (3 small)
5 oz. (150 g) celery root
2 Roseval potatoes
$^2/_3$ cup (3 ½ oz./100 g) peas
6 Little Gem lettuces
1 tomato
2 tablespoons vinaigrette

In a pan of boiling water, cook the eggs for 9 minutes. (It is important to respect this time to keep the yolk slightly soft.) Set aside.

Make the mayonnaise (for a nice emulsion, your ingredients should be at room temperature). In a bowl, whisk the egg yolk with the mustard. Season with salt and pepper and add the vinegar. Keep whisking while gradually pouring in the oil so that the mayonnaise thickens. Refrigerate.

Prepare the vegetables. Peel the carrots, celery root, and potatoes, then dice them finely. Cook them separately in a large pan of boiling salted water. Finish by cooking the peas. Allow 3–6 minutes cooking time, depending on the vegetables. To ensure that they remain slightly crunchy, refresh the cooked vegetables in a bowl of cold water and ice cubes. Set aside.

Mix this vegetable macédoine with a little of the mayonnaise and place two spoonfuls on each plate. Shell the hard-boiled eggs and cut them in half. Thin the remaining mayonnaise slightly with 1–2 teaspoons of water. Place three egg halves on the macédoine and coat each with mayonnaise to cover the whites. Thinly slice the Little Gem hearts and arrange them between the egg halves. Cut the tomato flesh into thin strips and arrange on top of the macédoine. Drizzle over a little vinaigrette and add a few grinds of pepper.

Enjoy with a Fleurie "Domaine Anita" 2017 by Anita Kuenel.

LEEK WHITES
WITH RAVIGOTE SAUCE

Ingredients

4 leeks
12 slices of white bread
3 ½ tablespoons (1 ¾ oz./50 g) butter

FOR THE RAVIGOTE SAUCE:
3 chives
3 chervil sprigs
1 dill sprig
1 basil sprig

2 shallots
4 teaspoons (20 ml) balsamic vinegar
½ tablespoon Meaux
(or whole-grain) mustard
Scant ½ cup (100 ml) hazelnut oil
Scant ½ cup (100 ml) sunflower oil
Salt and freshly ground pepper

SERVES 6

▪

PREP: 20 MINUTES
COOK: 15 MINUTES

▪

Make the ravigote sauce. Finely chop the chives, chervil, dill, and basil. Peel and finely chop the shallots. Pour the vinegar into a bowl, add a pinch of salt, and leave to dissolve. Stir in the mustard and a grind of pepper. Gradually pour in the hazelnut and sunflower oils, while whisking continuously, then stir in the chopped herbs and shallots.

Cut the leeks in half lengthwise and rinse several times to remove any dirt. Cut into regular lengths, keeping only the white, then steam for 10 minutes.

Dice the bread into small croutons. In a skillet, brown them for a few minutes in the butter. Pat dry with paper towels.

Arrange the warm leeks in the center of each plate, gently stir the ravigote sauce, and pour a spoonful over each plate. Sprinkle over some croutons and add a grind of pepper.

Enjoy with a dry Jurançon "Clos Uroulat" 2013 by Charles Hours.

A FINE TEAM

Crowned with a rich heritage and now a benchmark for French art de vivre, La Fontaine de Mars is a veritable institution.

At lunchtime and in the evening, lively conversations match the pace of the dishes coming and going from the kitchens, and diners seem to be delighting in a multitude of things at once. Among them are government ministers, movie and rock stars, captains of industry, and designers, all enchanted by La Fontaine de Mars' informal and friendly atmosphere. Leaving their celebrity trappings in the cloakroom while they dine, they happily surrender to the pleasure of having a good time.

It should be said that the restaurant's owner watches over the well-being of her guests with the attention of a mother caring for her children. Christiane Boudon has been the life and soul of the restaurant since she first arrived here and drew aside the curtain to greet a roomful of diners she needed to win over. During opening hours, her cheerful voice can be heard from table to table as she moves around the restaurant, greeting each diner with a kind, friendly word. Noon and night, as soon as the doors open, her warm handshakes and spontaneous embraces make everyone feel at home here.

She may take center stage, but she leads a whole team in her wake—a close-knit community of men and women, many of whom have been faithful to her for a long time.

Fabrice Régnault, the restaurant manager, has been here for twenty-five years; while her faithful headwaiters Laurent Bonnivard and Grégory Michel have been here seventeen and Michel Sousa ten years. These four loyal teammates arrived here young, completed their training with her, and over the years have become almost like part of the restaurant's family. When questioned about their loyalty to La Fontaine de Mars, all speak of an unrivaled working atmosphere, a feeling of complete trust, a true family spirit, and the pleasure of serving regulars with whom they've created a real rapport over the years. Virtually every day, they have the chance to warmly greet and catch up with a variety of regulars, as we might with old friends who we don't see very often but who remain dear to us.

When things get busy and it's all hands on deck, the team takes to the floor with a certain excitement and the sense that they have a lot to live up to—a bit like in the theater, where, night after night, each performance is like the first time. In the kitchen as in the dining room, a team spirit energizes everyone, galvanizing them to give the best of themselves and carry out their tasks with enthusiasm for hours on end. Once calm has descended again, after a last lap of the dining room, the gratifying feeling of having made people happy brings a smile to the team's faces. The red curtain then falls back into place until the next performance, when everything will start up again.

SEMI-COOKED DUCK
FOIE GRAS TERRINE

SERVES 6
■
PREP: 30 MINUTES
REST: 48 HOURS
COOK: 40 MINUTES
■

Ingredients

2 ¼ lb. (1 kg) raw duck foie gras
1 tablespoon salt
¾ teaspoon freshly ground pepper
Pinch of potassium nitrate
Pinch of superfine sugar
Scant ½ cup (100 ml) Monbazillac
Fleur de sel

Two days before you want to serve it, ask your butcher for some very fresh lobes of foie gras. Open them carefully and, with a knife, gently remove all the small nerves and blood vessels. Lay the lobes flat in a rectangular dish, the deveined part on top.

In a bowl, mix the salt, pepper, potassium nitrate, sugar, and Monbazillac, then, with your hands, spread this mixture on top of the lobes of foie gras. Cover with plastic wrap and refrigerate for 24 hours.

The next day, place the foie gras into a 1-quart (1-kg) terrine dish, laying the seasoned side of the lobes against the edges of the dish, with the smooth side on top. Preheat the oven to 210°F (100°C). Cover the terrine with foil and bake for about 40 minutes. Check it is cooked by sticking a probe into the center: remove the terrine from the oven when the temperature registers 115°F (46°C).

Remove the foil and allow to cool. Then place a small board covered with foil over the terrine and place a small weight (a can, for example) on top to press lightly and cause the fat to rise to the surface. After about 20 minutes, refrigerate the foie gras and leave overnight.

Remove the small board, smooth the layer of fat over the top of the terrine with a spatula and, with a knife, lightly criss-cross the surface. Remove the fat from around the terrine and gently melt this in a small saucepan. Strain it through a sieve and pour it gently over the top of the terrine to cover it with an even layer of fat.

Refrigerate the foie gras for 6 hours to allow the aromas to develop perfectly. When ready to serve, cut it into thick slices, add a pinch of fleur de sel and serve with toasted country bread.

Enjoy with a Sauternes "Château de Fargues" 2007 by Lur Saluces or, more originally, with a Pauillac "Château Latour" 2016.

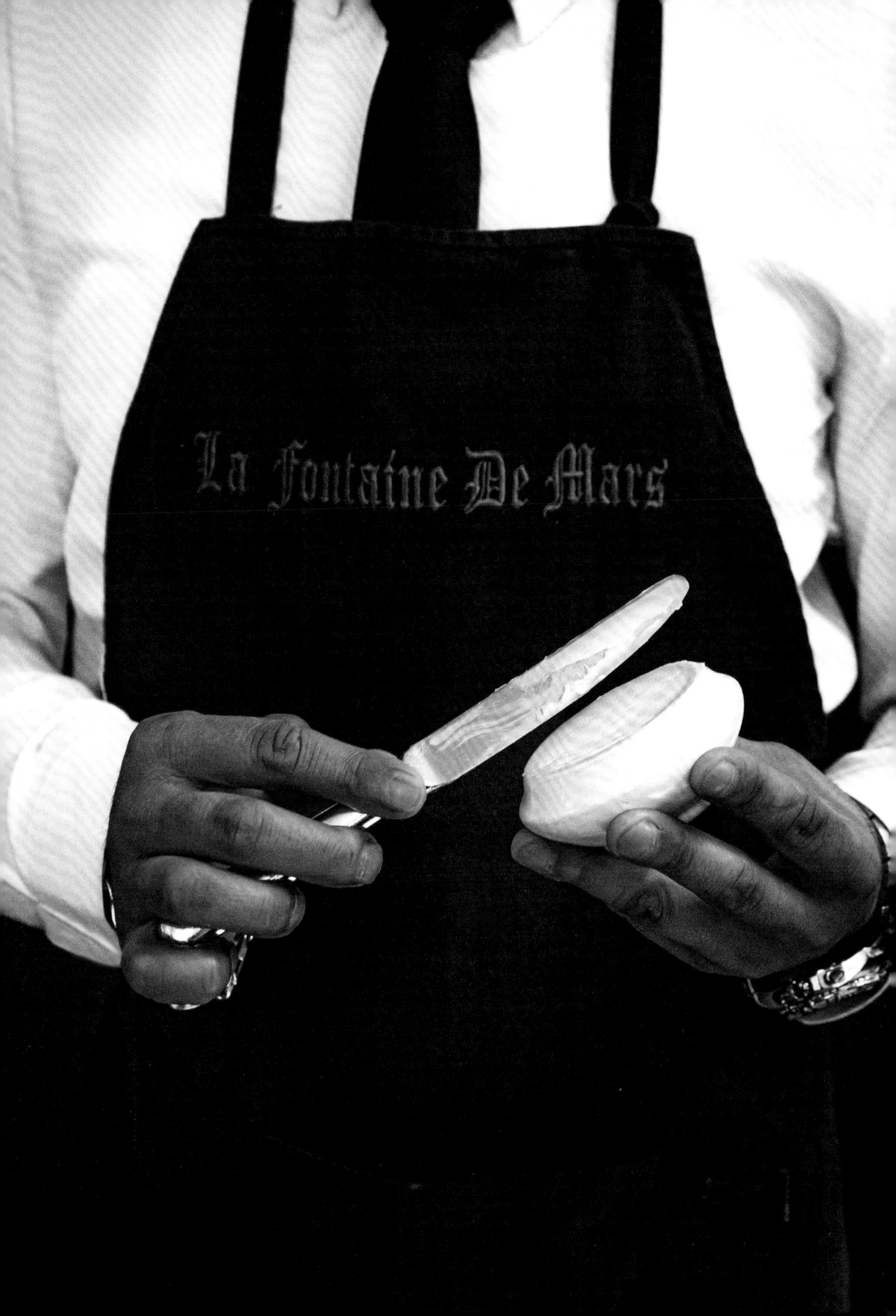
La Fontaine De Mars

CREAM OF PUMPKIN SOUP
WITH HOT FOIE GRAS

Ingredients

2 ¼ lb. (1 kg) pumpkin flesh
½ onion
½ carrot
1 tablespoon olive oil
4 teaspoons (¾ oz./20 g) butter
2 cups (500 ml) chicken bouillon
2 cups (500 ml) whipping cream
Salt and pepper
8 ½ oz. (240 g) raw foie gras

SERVES 6

■

PREP: 20 MINUTES
COOK: 55 MINUTES

■

Make the soup. Choose a nice orange pumpkin—not too big or the flesh may be stringy. Cut the pumpkin in half and scoop out the seeds. Chop the pumpkin flesh. Dice the onion and carrot. In a pan, sweat the onion and carrot in the oil and butter without coloring, then add the pumpkin. Pour in the chicken bouillon, bring to a boil, and simmer for 45 minutes. Check that the pumpkin is cooked by sticking a knife in it. Turn off the heat and, while the soup is still hot, puree it using a stick blender. Place the pan back on the heat and stir in the cream. Season with salt and pepper. Bring to a simmer than strain the soup through a fine mesh sieve. Keep it warm.

Make the hot foie gras. Heat a knife blade by dipping it in boiling water, then cut the foie gras into thick slices. Season with salt and pepper. Heat a grill pan and add the slices of foie gras. Turn them over and check that they are cooked by poking a piece of raw spaghetti into a slice: it shouldn't break.

Just before serving, pour the hot soup into soup bowls and carefully place a slice of panfried foie gras on top of each serving.

Enjoy with a Saint-Aubin Premier Cru
"Les Murgers des Dents de Chien" 2016 by Alex Gambal.

RABBIT TERRINE
WITH FOIE GRAS

SERVES 6

PREP: 1 HOUR
REST: 12 HOURS
COOK:
1 HOUR 30 MINUTES

Ingredients

7 oz. (200 g) rabbit meat
2 sheets of gelatin
⅓ cup (80 ml) white wine
2 ½ oz. (70 g) raw chicken fillet
2 ½ oz. (70 g) fatty bacon
3 ½ oz. (100 g) duck foie gras
1 shallot
¼ oz. (7 g) tarragon (about
2 tablespoons chopped leaves)

¼ oz. (7 g) rosemary (about
1 tablespoon chopped leaves)
½ oz. (15 g) black truffle
¼ cup (30 g) shelled pistachios
Pinch of garlic
Pinch of thyme
½ tablespoon salt
½ teaspoon pepper
7 oz. (200 g) caul fat, soaked in
a mixture of vinegar and water
12 vine leaves

The day before, ask your butcher to bone some rabbit legs to give you 7 oz. (200 g) of meat.

Soften the gelatin sheets in a bowl of cold water for 3 minutes. In a saucepan, heat the white wine and add the drained gelatin. Stir in and leave to cool. Set aside the white wine jelly in the fridge.

Dice the rabbit meat, chicken fillet, bacon, and foie gras. Refrigerate.

Finely chop the shallot, tarragon, and rosemary. Chop the black truffle. Crush the pistachios. Crush the garlic. Mix all these ingredients together in a large bowl, then stir in the thyme and the diced meats. Mix gently with your hands, then mix in the white wine jelly. Season with salt and pepper.

Preheat the oven to 200°F (90°C). Moisten the bottom and edges of a 1-quart (1-kg) terrine mold with cold water. Drain the caul fat then use it to line the mold. Spread the vine leaves over the caul fat, leaving them to hang over the edge of the mold by about 1 ½ inches (4 cm). Fill the mold with the meat mixture, gently pressing it down into the mold with your hand. Fold the vine leaves over the top, then the caul fat. Cover the terrine with foil and bake for at least 1 hour 30 minutes, until a probe inserted in the center registers 143°F (62°C).

Remove the foil and allow to cool. Cover the terrine with a small board and place a heavy weight (a can, for example) on top, to compress the terrine. Refrigerate overnight.

The next day, serve the rabbit terrine cut into thick slices, accompanied with toasted country bread and onion relish, for example.

Enjoy with a dry Jurançon "Sève d'Automne" 2014 by Henri Ramonteu.

■

FIRST STEPS

The story of Christiane Boudon's involvement with La Fontaine de Mars began in August 1989, when the young woman was walking along the Rue Saint-Dominique, in the 7th arrondissement of Paris, on a stifling hot day. There, she was enchanted by a house standing under archways facing a splendid and impressive fountain. The quaint charm of the house, which was closed up for the summer, immediately appealed to her. As she approached the building, irresistibly drawn by the blanc d'Espagne finish on the windows, she had an intuition that her life would be here. So strong was this conviction that, right then and there, she decided to buy the establishment with her husband, Jacques. Both were already in the hotel and restaurant business.

Having graduated from the hotel management school in Toulouse, Christiane had moved "up" to Paris to lead a brilliant career. As a child, her favorite pastime had been playing shops, and she soon grew to love contact with real customers and would give anything to be able to lend a hand in her mother's electrical goods store or her aunt's seed store. A few years later, she was dreaming of managing a luxury hotel and was convinced that this was where her future lay. No sooner had she arrived in Paris, than she was taken on at the Hôtel Scribe, where, she imagined, a fine future lay ahead of her. But fate had other plans. The Hôtel Nikko's restaurant manager, whom she had sought out for professional advice, suggested she turn to the restaurant industry, believing that she had all the qualities necessary to excel

there. He consequently offered her a place in the hotel's brasserie. It was an offer she couldn't refuse. The recent memory of Joel Robuchon was still evident in Nikko's kitchens, where his sous-chefs Jacky Fréau and Jacques Sénéchal had taken over the reins, with Jean-Paul Hévin presiding as pastry chef.

It was an ambitious challenge and Christiane threw herself into the work body and soul—and has never looked back. There was no time to remind herself that she already knew the role like the back of her hand, that she had an instinctive feel for it. Although she was a night owl, she began at dawn, but without her body clock suffering the slightest disruption. The passion she put into her work was a powerful stimulant, and everything went swimmingly with the cosmopolitan clientele, whom she greeted in many languages. She was perfectly in her element. Nikko's prophetic manager had been right. She progressed quickly and soon became head waiter of the Michelin-starred restaurant.

But, keen to learn and experience more, she was feeling the need for a new challenge. On a whim, she replied to a Burger King advertisement. Was it the foolhardiness of youth that led her to leave a Michelin-starred restaurant for a fast food one? Or was it simply the desire to know everything there was to know about the profession she's so passionate about? Once again, she threw herself into the new role, keeping up with the tough tasks and the hectic pace. She learned a huge amount. However, she was increasingly homesick for the South-West and she ended up quitting her job, with the firm intention of leaving Paris, too. But once again, fate intervened and hijacked her plans.

LANDAISE SALAD
WITH DRIED DUCK BREAST

Ingredients

FOR THE DRIED DUCK BREAST:
1 duck breast weighing at
least 1 lb. 5 oz. (600 g)
⅓ cup (2 ¾ oz./80 g) coarse gray salt
¼ teaspoon superfine sugar
¼ teaspoon fine salt
¼ teaspoon Espelette pepper
½ bay leaf
Leaves from 1 thyme sprig
Pinch of crushed garlic
Freshly ground pepper

FOR THE LANDAISE SALAD:
1 tablespoon Dijon mustard
1 tablespoon sherry vinegar
2 tablespoons sunflower oil
2 tablespoons hazelnut oil
Mesclun leaves
8 ½ oz. (240 g) cooked green beans
(about 2 cups cut into 1-inch/
2.5-cm lengths)
3 tablespoons toasted pine nuts
2 confit duck legs
Croutons rubbed with garlic
Salt and pepper

SERVES 6

■

PREP: 30 MINUTES
REST: 1 MONTH

■

Prepare the dried duck breast. A month before you want to serve it, order a good-quality duck breast from your butcher. In a bowl, stir together the coarse salt, sugar, fine salt, and Espelette pepper, then stir in the bay leaf, thyme, and garlic. Rub the duck breast with this mixture and refrigerate for 24 hours.

Rinse the duck breast in clear water, dry it well in a clean kitchen towel, then cover it completely with a layer of freshly ground pepper. Thread a length of kitchen string through the layer of fat at one end of the duck breast and hang it in a dark, dry place for 10 days.

Untie the duck breast, wrap it in a clean cotton kitchen towel, and leave it to dry out in the fridge for at least three weeks so that the seasoning spreads throughout the flesh.

Make the landaise salad. Make a vinaigrette with the mustard, vinegar and oil and pour it over the mesclun leaves. Divide the salad between the plates, then sprinkle with the toasted pine nuts, a few shreds of duck confit and the croutons. Cut the dried duck breast into thin slices and arrange them on the salad.

Enjoy with a Vosne-Romanée Village "Domaine Arnoux-Lachaux" 2014.

A SPECTACULAR TURN OF EVENTS

On Thursday, February 6, 1986, a few days before she was due to take the train to Tarbes (in southwestern France), one of Christiane's friends invited her to drink hot chocolate with a friend whose parents ran a café near the Pont de l'Alma. The friend's name was Jacques Boudon and Christiane never left for her beloved South-West. Although she at first found this young man quite loathsome, it wasn't long before she couldn't bear to be without him. For their first dinner date, they went to La Coupole, where the young woman, no doubt a little overwhelmed, ordered a steak tartare, despite hating raw meat! Nevertheless, it was here, in this famous brasserie, that they declared their love for each other—and sealed their fate. From then on, they teamed up for the better, and it wasn't long before they were putting their complementary skills to work to realize their shared dream.

Jacques Boudon was an insider. With roots in Aveyron on his mother's side and Lozère on his father's, he is descended from the "Auvergnats de Paris" (or bougnats—people from the rural Massif Central area of France who moved to Paris, where many ran cafés, both selling drinks and delivering coal) and is proud of his roots. His father had moved "up" to Paris in the 1950s to work at his sister's café, while his mother was the daughter of a coal merchant in the Paris suburbs. After their marriage, they opened the Alma tobacconist's, where their son Jacques later took his first steps.

As a young man, Jacques studied at business school before training as a chef at a Michelin-starred restaurant, Ma Cuisine, located in Paris's 17th arrondissement. He learned everything at this highly disciplined school, then joined the family business, serving simple, good-quality lunches. He worked there for a few years and gained solid experience, all the while dreaming of one day running his own business.

THE DREAM TAKES SHAPE

When Jacques and Christiane got married in 1988, they instinctively knew that they would combine their love for each other with their passion for their work. At the time, they didn't know where and how, but they used to roam the beautiful neighborhoods of Paris with an eye on the lookout for a suitable place. It was at this point that their paths crossed that of La Fontaine de Mars, then closed for the summer. It was 1989, and it so happened that the Launays, who had reached retirement age, were wanting to sell their establishment. But the young couple had to wait a further two years before they were able to finally sign the deed of sale.

When at last they held the keys of La Fontaine de Mars in their hands, their elation was mixed with apprehension at the enormity of the challenge they had taken on. They were going to have to roll up their sleeves and get to work to wake this sleeping beauty.

For the interior design, the Boudons looked to Michel Lafond, who trained with Damas and Slavik, responsible for some of the finest

brasseries in Paris. Lafond's reputation was well established among the small bougnat world in Paris. They were given the best advice: to leave the decor as it was to preserve the heart and soul of the place. As chef, Jacques Boudon chose Éric Lefèvre, who had trained in a three-Michelin-starred restaurant before becoming a sous-chef in another acclaimed establishment. Without completely reworking the menu, he brought a certain refinement to it with the aim of attracting a new clientele. Changes were introduced gradually, in line with the wishes of the young couple, who felt that the restaurant deserved to be treated with gentleness and respect. History has shown their instinctive decision to have been a wise one.

A FULL HOUSE

Once the work began, locals started to get jittery, wondering what the fate of "their" Fontaine de Mars was going to be. Some had been visiting the restaurant since childhood and were eagerly awaiting its rebirth to continue weaving the memories the place held for them. It was important not to disappoint them. The restaurant was to be completely renovated and would be restored to its former glory thanks to the skills of specialist craftsmen, who managed to recreate some of the furniture with the patina of the old. Hence, despite being fresh out of the workshops, some of the copper on the bar and certain display and storage cabinets seem to be aged by time and to have seen much life already. In just a few months, La Fontaine de Mars managed to regain its youth without denying anything of its past.

As soon as the doors opened on April 15, 1992—on the dot of midday—the restaurant filled up as though by magic and, within minutes, every table was taken. The opening was a triumph, and over the following days and weeks, the success of the restaurant—which was constantly full—was established. Journalists, enchanted by the place, praised it in such prestigious publications as Figaroscope and Elle. The phone didn't stop ringing. The original small team was soon overwhelmed by events. It was time to expand. Young people from very different backgrounds arrived to reinforce the kitchen and serving staff, and everyone got up to speed, swept along by Christiane Boudon's extraordinary energy. They gave the restaurant their all, and everything came together wonderfully. The number of foreign customers was growing, Patricia Wells had returned to her red moleskin banquette, and grandmothers came to meet their grandchildren here at lunchtime. Meanwhile the group of veteran cavalry officers, many of whom had been in the Resistance, who had been dining at the same table every Thursday since just after the War, soon resumed their weekly ritual. Returning customers also included students from the nearby American university and expatriates housed in the neighborhood, as well as a string of US ambassadors, who regularly dined here during their time in Paris. To these regulars were added people from the fashion world with hearty appetites. Observing this general enthusiasm, it was clear to Jacques and Christiane that their gamble had well and truly paid off.

AUBRAC BEEF TARTARE

SERVES 6

·

PREP: 30 MINUTES

·

Ingredients

6 tablespoons Dijon mustard
6 egg yolks
1 scant cup (200 ml) sunflower oil
1 scant cup (200 ml) olive oil
5 tablespoons tomato ketchup
Worcestershire sauce
Tabasco
Generous 1 cup (5 oz./150 g) finely chopped shallots
Generous 1 cup (5 oz./150 g) finely chopped onion

Generous 1 cup (5 oz./150 g) drained and chopped pickled gherkins
½ bunch of basil, chopped
½ bunch of flat-leaf parsley, chopped ½ cup (1 ¾ oz./50 g) capers in vinegar, drained (reserve a few for garnishing)
2 ¼ lb. (1 kg) Aubrac beef—ask your butcher to mince some very fresh tender lean steak
Salt and freshly ground pepper

In a large bowl, mix together the mustard and egg yolks, then gradually whisk in the sunflower and olive oils to make a mayonnaise. Stir in the ketchup. Season with salt, pepper, Worcestershire sauce, and Tabasco to taste.

Stir in the shallots, onion, gherkins, basil, parsley, and capers. Place the bowl on crushed ice then add the minced beef and mix in well.

Place a portion of beef tartare on each of six chilled plates and garnish with the reserved capers. Sprinkle over some salt and a grind of pepper. Serve with very crisp homemade fries and a mixture of young salad leaves drizzled with olive oil.

Enjoy with a Morgon "Côte du Py" 2016 by Jean Foillard.

SNAILS
À LA FONTAINE

SERVES 6

·

PREP: 1 HOUR
COOK: 35 MINUTES

·

Ingredients

1 garlic clove
1 ½ cups (12 ½ oz./350 g) butter
1 bunch of flat-leaf parsley
2 ¾ tablespoons Meaux
(or whole-grain) mustard
¾ teaspoon fine salt
2 ¾ tablespoons ground almonds
1 1¼ oz. (35 g) porcini mushrooms

1 tablespoon olive oil
4 teaspoons (¾ oz./20 g) butter
1 ¾ oz. (50 g) cured ham
1 ¾ oz. (50 g) shallots
(about ¼ cup finely chopped)
36 Burgundy snails without
their shells

Croutons rubbed with garlic
Salt and pepper

Preheat the oven to 280°F (140°C).

Cut the garlic clove in half and remove the germ. Blanch the garlic then crush it. Beat the 1 ½cups (12 ½ oz./350 g) butter until soft, then add the crushed garlic, chopped parsley, mustard, salt, and ground almonds.

Wash the mushrooms, chop finely, and fry in the olive oil and 2 teaspoons of the butter. Leave to cool. Finely dice the cured ham then blanch it. Leave to cool. Chop the shallots and fry them in the remaining 2 teaspoons of butter over low heat until soft.

Carefully stir together the herb butter, the mushrooms, ham, and shallots until combined.

Drain the snails and dry them thoroughly with paper towels so that they don't burst during cooking. Put them in snail dishes and cover generously with the herb butter.

Cook the snails for about 15 minutes, until they begin to bubble. Serve immediately with toast and salted butter.

Enjoy with a white Santenay "Domaine Girardin" 2015 by Vincent Girardin.

At the helm, the couple made a dream team, their lives organized around the pace of the restaurant twenty-four hours a day. Every day, they closed the restaurant curtain at two o'clock in the morning, exhausted but happy. Christiane led the dining-room staff, while Jacques devoted himself to the restaurant's organization and, very soon, to its evolution. He was the restaurant's mastermind, constantly challenging his imagination to satisfy its ever-growing clientele and ensure it maintained its standards of excellence. Their complementarity was their strength.

AN INTERNATIONAL AURA

The 1990s passed like a dream, with signs of trust and recognition pouring in from all sides. In 1991, in her book Paris Bistro Cooking, American journalist Linda Dannenberg distinguished La Fontaine de Mars as one of the finest bistros in Paris. The repercussions were felt immediately: a new clientele flocked to the restaurant. In addition to this success, the restaurant received several distinctions. In 1993, La Fontaine de Mars was awarded the prize for best bistro in Paris by the Lebey guide and, in 1998, the Pudlo guide named Christiane Boudon the best hostess of the year.

In the wake of this current of unanimous favor from the press and food critics, the restaurant's renown spread not only throughout Paris but around the world. Many languages now resounded within the walls of La Fontaine de Mars.

In 1998, the first Brazilians came, on a visit to support their team at the World Cup. Between two games, broadcast a stone's throw away on the Champ-de-Mars, they came to La Fontaine de Mars to recover their emotions around a cassoulet, the French equivalent of their famous feijoada cooked with black beans and pork. Mexicans, also fans of cassoulet, followed suit not long afterward, as did Japanese, who would even order this hearty dish on the hottest of summer days.

Many customers from the United States, Asia, and other far-off locations would cross La Fontaine de Mars's threshold for the first time with the restaurant's menu already firmly established in their mind. Judging from the assurance with which they placed their order, one would assume that they were already perfectly familiar with snails, duck confit, trout meunière, œufs à la neige, or rum baba. Some were following the express recommendation of a Korean, American, or Japanese magazine. Others preferred to rely on word-of-mouth, an impressive medium that operates even at great distance. Like the elegant Australian who, barely seated, ordered hot foie gras and a green salad, to be followed by a floating island dessert. Her dentist, whom she had visited the day before flying to Paris, had recommended that she dine at La Fontaine de Mars. The amiable practitioner had even taken the trouble to advise her on the menu.

GRAND CASSOULET
WITH TARBES BEANS

SERVES 6-8

PREP: 1 HOUR 30 MINUTES
REST: 24 HOURS
COOK:
4 HOURS 20 MINUTES

Ingredients

4 ⅓ cups (1 ¾ lb./800 g) dry Tarbes beans
2 tablespoons (30 g) duck fat
Generous 1 cup (5 oz./150 g)
finely chopped onion
Generous 1 cup (5 oz./150 g)
finely chopped carrots
1 cup (5 oz./150 g) diced cured ham
10 ½ cups (2.5 L) duck stock
2 tsp. tomato paste
5 oz. (150 g) pork crackling, diced
1 cured ham bone

1 bouquet garni
1 ½ oz. (40 g) cured ham fat
2 garlic cloves, crushed
2 tomatoes
⅓ cup (1 ¾ oz./50 g) toasted pine nuts
½ bunch of basil, chopped
Scant ¼ cup (50 ml) olive oil
6 duck confits
2 1/4 lb. (1 kg) firm-fleshed potatoes
1 lb. 5 oz. (600 g) Toulouse sausages
(see recipe on page 58)
6 thick slices of garlic sausage
Salt and pepper

The day before, put the dry Tarbes beans beans in a bowl, cover with cold water, and refrigerate for 24 hours.

The next day, melt the duck fat in a large cooking pot and sauté the onion. Add the carrot and sweat well. At the last minute, add the ham, taking care not to let it brown. Drain and add the beans. Stir. Pour in the duck stock to cover the beans by 2 inches (5 cm). Add the tomato paste, crackling, ham bone, and bouquet garni. Simmer for 3 hours, stirring regularly.

Blend the ham fat with the garlic and add this mixture to the beans 15 minutes before the end of the cooking time. Season with salt and pepper (avoid doing so earlier to prevent the beans becoming tough). Keep warm.

Peel, core, and seed the tomatoes, then crush them. In a bowl, mix together the tomato, pine nuts, basil, and olive oil. Set aside.

Preheat the oven to 350°F (170°C). Slice the potatoes thickly (so they don't dry out while cooking) and lay the slices in a roasting pan. Place the duck confits, skin side up, on top and roast in the oven for 30 minutes. Fry the Toulouse sausages and garlic sausage in a skillet. Keep warm.

Put all the meat in a casserole dish and cover with the beans. Top with the crushed tomato mixture. Grind plenty of pepper over the top of the cassoulet and cook in the oven at 325°F (160°C) for about 20 minutes, until the top is slightly crispy and everything is simmering gently. Serve immediately.

Enjoy with a Madiran "Château Montus Prestige" 2013 magnum by Alain Brumont.

LEG OF LAMB
WITH GRATIN DAUPHINOIS

SERVES 6

∙

PREP: 1 HOUR
REST: 24 HOURS
COOKING: 3 HOURS

∙

Ingredients

FOR THE LEG OF LAMB:
4 tablespoons olive oil
3 tablespoons (1 ½ oz./45 g)
Dijon mustard
1 thyme sprig
3 garlic cloves
2 ½ lb. (1.2 kg) leg of milk-fed Lozère
lamb, boned and tied by your butcher
1 tablespoon white wine
Scant ½ cup (100 ml) chicken bouillon
1 tablespoon water

1 tablespoon vinegar mustard
1 tablespoon (15 g) butter

FOR THE GRATIN DAUPHINOIS:
1 ¾ lb. (800 g) firm-fleshed potatoes
2 cups (500 ml) whipping cream
2 cups (500 ml) milk
1 garlic clove
Scant ⅓ cup (1 oz./30 g) grated
emmenthal cheese
Salt and pepper

Prepare the leg of lamb. The day before, mix 3 tablespoons of the olive oil and mustard together in a bowl, then add the thyme leaves and crushed garlic cloves. Massage the lamb with this mixture and wrap it in plastic wrap. Refrigerate for 24 hours so that the aromas are diffused throughout the meat.

The next day prepare the gratin dauphinois. Preheat the oven to 300°F (150°C). Peel the potatoes, slice them ½ inch (1.5 cm) thick, and place in a baking dish. In a bowl, stir together the cream and the milk, then add the crushed garlic. Season with salt and pepper. Pour over the potatoes, cover the dish with foil, and cook for 1 hour 40 minutes. Remove the foil, scatter the grated cheese over the potatoes, and brown in the oven for 30 minutes. Keep warm.

Adjust the oven control to 325°F (160°C). In a skillet, brown the leg of lamb in the remaining olive oil, place it in a roasting pan, and roast for 40 minutes, until a probe inserted in the center registers 118°F (48°C). Turn off the oven, wrap the lamb in foil, and let it rest in the oven with the door open, so that the meat is perfectly tender.

Deglaze the roasting pan with the white wine to loosen all the cooking residues from the bottom of the pan, then stir in the bouillon, water, and mustard. Strain this gravy through a fine mesh sieve into a small saucepan and, over low heat, whisk in the butter.

Carve the leg of lamb into thick slices and arrange on hot plates. Pour over the gravy and serve with the gratin dauphinois.

Enjoy with a Lalande-de-Pomerol "La Fleur de Boüard" 2010 by Hubert de Boüard.

HOMEMADE TOULOUSE SAUSAGE
WITH SPLIT-PEA PUREE

SERVES 6

·

PREP: 40 MINUTES
REST: 24 HOURS
COOK: 1 HOUR 10 MINUTES

·

Ingredients

FOR THE SAUSAGES:
16 ft. (5 m) natural casing
1 lb. 4 oz. (550 g) pork shoulder
8 ¾ oz. (250 g) pork throat
1 oz. (25 g) cured ham fat
2 ¼ oz. (60 g) pork crackling
2 ¼ oz. (60 g) caramelized shallots
Pinch of grated nutmeg
2 teaspoons fine salt
½ teaspoon pepper
¼ teaspoon Espelette pepper
2 shallots, finely chopped
1 tablespoon olive oil
Scant ¼ cup (50 ml) white wine

FOR THE SPLIT-PEA PUREE:
½ onion
1 clove
1 ½ cups (10 ½ oz./300 g) split peas
1 carrot
1 bouquet garni
1 tablespoon olive oil
1 ¼ cups (300 ml) whipping cream
1 tablespoon (15 g) butter
Salt and pepper

Make the sausages. The day before, put the casing in a bowl of cold water and let soak for 24 hours in the refrigerator. The next day, mince the pork shoulder, throat, and rind, the cured ham fat, the shallots, and nutmeg in a meat grinder. Stir this stuffing by hand to thoroughly combine, then stir in the salt, pepper, and Espelette pepper. Fill the sausages: for this, use a sausage stuffer attachment on the meat grinder to get the stuffing into the casing.

Make the split-pea puree. Stud the onion with the clove and put in a saucepan of boiling water with the split peas, carrot, and bouquet garni. Cook for 50 minutes, or until the split peas are very tender. Drain the split peas and reserve the cooking liquid. Puree the split peas with a little of their cooking liquid, then add the olive oil, cream, and butter. Season with salt and pepper. Keep warm.

Prick the raw sausage with a fork so that it doesn't burst when cooking and fry it with the chopped shallots in the olive oil in a skillet over medium heat for 20 minutes. Remove the sausage from the pan and cut it into thick pieces. Deglaze the pan with the wine and one ladle of the reserved cooking liquid, then keep this gravy hot.

To serve, place the homemade Toulouse sausage on warm plates, pour over a little gravy, and add some split-pea puree.

Enjoy with a Saint-Joseph "Terre d'Encres" 2015 by Georges Vernay.

HOMEMADE DUCK CONFIT

SERVES 6

■

PREP: 20 MINUTES
REST: 24 HOURS
COOK:
3 HOURS 40 MINUTES

■

Ingredients

½ cup (4 ¼ oz./120 g) Guérande
coarse sea salt
½ bay leaf, cut into strips
1 ½ tablespoons (½oz./15 g)
cracked pepper
2 pinches of Espelette pepper
6 fattened duck legs

8 cups (2 L) duck fat
1 lb. 2 oz. (500 g) Noirmoutier potatoes
3 garlic cloves
1 tablespoon olive oil
3 parsley sprigs, finely chopped

The day before, mix the coarse salt, bay leaf, cracked pepper, and Espelette pepper together in a bowl. Rub the fleshy side of the duck legs with this mixture then refrigerate for 24 hours.

The next day, preheat the oven to 200°F (90°C). Rinse the duck legs and dry them with a clean kitchen towel. Place the duck legs in a casserole and cover with the duck fat (reserve 1 tablespoon for the potatoes) then confit in the oven for about 2 hours 30 minutes. To check they are cooked, press a piece of raw spaghetti into the flesh: it shouldn't break. The duck confit can be stored covered with duck fat in a sealed jar in a dark place for up to 3 months.

Preheat the oven to 325°F (165°C). Rub the potatoes with salt to clean them, then put them in a baking dish with two of the garlic cloves (don't peel them but score them by making several small cuts along the sides to allow the aromas to diffuse), the oil, and the reserved duck fat. Roast the potatoes for about 30 minutes, turning them regularly. Check they are cooked by sticking a knife in one. When the potatoes are cool enough to touch, cut them into thick slices.

To prevent the duck flesh from drying out, place the legs in a baking dish on top of the sliced potato and cook in the oven for about 35 minutes. The skin of the duck will turn a nice caramel color.

Just before serving, drain the potatoes and fry them over high heat with the remaining garlic clove, crushed, and the chopped parsley.

Serve the duck confit on warm plates with the potatoes and some curly endive seasoned with a sherry-vinegar vinaigrette.

Enjoy with a Bordeaux Supérieur "Reignac" 2011 by Yves Vatelot, served at room temperature.

Terrine de gibier en saison

PIERRE'S HARE "À LA ROYALE"

Ingredients

SERVES 6

•

PREP: 4 HOURS
REST: 18 HOURS
COOK: 16 HOURS

•

1 cured ham hock
1 good hare, prepared by your butcher
1 bouquet garni
3 tablespoon olive oil
3 bottles of Monbazillac
1 ¾ oz. (50 g) of white sliced bread
(1 large slice)
3 tablespoons whole milk
1 lb. 2 oz. (500 g) lamb sweetbreads
3 eggs
6 juniper berries
Pinch of grated nutmeg
1 clove
Pinch of ground cinnamon
½ teaspoon black pepper
2 tablespoons rum
¼ bunch of parsley
2 ½ teaspoons fine salt

1 ¼ cups (6 ¼ oz./180 g) finely chopped shallots
2 tablespoons (30 g) butter
3 ½ oz. (100 g) porcini mushrooms
(1 ⅓ cups chopped)
¾ oz. (20 g) black truffle (¼ cup chopped)
3 ½ oz. (100 g) carrots
⅔ cup (3 ½ oz./100 g) diced cured ham
1 lobe of raw duck foie gras
1 lb. 2 oz. (500 g) caul fat, soaked in
a mixture of vinegar and water
3 ¼ tablespoons (1 ¾ oz./50 g) Dijon mustard
5 teaspoons (30 g) superfine sugar
A few thyme sprigs
Reserved hare blood
1 square of dark chocolate (optional)
Salt and pepper

The day before, place the ham hock in a bowl of cold water and refrigerate it overnight.

The next day, ask your butcher to prepare a hare (he will need to skin and gut it; reserve the offal, being careful of the bile; keep the blood by adding a drizzle of wine vinegar; and bone it flat without piercing the flesh).

Make the game stock. Add one tablespoon of the olive oil to a cooking pot and add the hare carcass and head, the flesh that remains on the bones, the desalted ham hock, and the bouquet garni. Pour in 2 bottles of of the Monbazillac and simmer over low heat for 1 hour 30 minutes, regularly skimming off the impurities. Set aside.

Make the stuffing. Soak the bread in the milk. In a saucepan, reduce the last bottle of Monbazillac until it is of a syrupy consistency. Leave to cool. Blanch the sweetbreads, chop them, then, in a bowl, mix with the milk-soaked bread, the eggs, spices, cooled Monbazillac syrup, rum, chopped parsley, offal, and salt. Refrigerate this stuffing.

Fry the shallots in the butter over low heat until caramelized. Peel, clean and dice the mushrooms, then fry them in one tablespoon of the olive oil until lightly colored. Remove the stuffing from the refrigerator and add the shallots, mushrooms, truffle, carrots, and cured ham. Refrigerate this stuffing.

Separate the lobes of foie gras and roll each in plastic wrap to make two identical rolls. They will form the heart of the stuffing.

Spread the hare out flat on the caul fat and shape it in to a rectangle. In a bowl, mix together the mustard, sugar, and thyme leaves, then brush this over the meat. Spread a layer of the stuffing mixture on top to about ½ inch (1.5 cm) thick. Unwrap the rolls of foie gras, lay them carefully down the center, and press them gently into the stuffing. Cover with the remaining stuffing, then carefully roll the stuffed hare into a ballotine. Wrap it in the caul fat, tie it up, then refrigerate it for at least 6 hours.

Preheat the oven to 200°F (90°C). In a casserole dish, brown the hare ballotine in one tablespoon of the olive oil over low heat. Skim off the cooking fat and pour in the game stock. Cook in the oven for 4 hours, basting regularly. Remove the ballotine from the casserole dish and, off the heat, stir the reserved blood into the sauce. Season with salt and pepper. If you wish, you can add a square of chocolate to tone down the strong flavor of the game.

Remove the string and cut the ballotine into thick slices. Pour the sauce onto the plates and place the slices of hare on top. Serve with pureed parsnips, for example.

Enjoy with a red Les Baux de Provence Chateau d'Estoublon
"Cuvée Mogador" 2013 by Valérie Reboul-Schneider.

FRICASSEE OF RABBIT
WITH MUSTARD, VEGETABLES, AND MACARONI

SERVES 6

PREP: 45 MINUTES
REST: 12 HOURS
COOK:
2 HOUR 30 MINUTES

Ingredients

6 Rex du Poitou rabbit legs, boned by
your butcher
2 tablespoons Dijon mustard
4 tablespoons olive oil
½ small garlic clove
1 thyme sprig

FOR THE GRAVY:
1 onion
1 shallot
2 carrots
3 garlic cloves
1 rabbit fronts, less the saddle, prepared
by your butcher
2 tablespoons olive oil

1 rosemary sprig
Scant ¼ cup (50 ml) white wine
3 1/3 cups (800 ml) chicken bouillon
1 tablespoon Meaux (or wholegrain) mustard
1 teaspoon Dijon mustard
Scant ¼ cup (50 ml) sherry vinegar
Salt and pepper

FOR THE VEGETABLES AND MACARONI:
5 oz. (150 g) green (French) beans (about
1 ½ cups cut into 1-inch/2.5-cm lengths)
5 oz. (150 g) pea pods (about 2 cups)
5 oz. (150 g) shelled peas (1 cup)
5 oz. (150 g) shelled fava beans (about 1 cup)
1 cup (3 ½ oz./100 g) macaroni

Prepare the rabbit. The day before, ask your butcher to prepare the rabbit fronts (remove the heart and lungs, then crush), which will be used to make the gravy, and to bone the forelegs (keep the carcasses, which will also be used in the gravy).

Cut the boneless legs into three, then brush them with the mustard and 2 tablespoons of the olive oil. Lay them in a baking dish, add the crushed garlic and the thyme leaves, cover with plastic wrap, and place in the fridge to marinate overnight.

The next day, make the gravy. Chop the shallot, onion, and carrot into large pieces and score the garlic cloves by making several small cuts along the sides. In a cooking pot, brown the carcasses and the crushed rabbit fronts in the olive oil,

then add the onion, shallot, carrots, garlic cloves, and rosemary. Cook until nicely browned. Drain everything in a colander, reserving the cooking fat. Wipe out the cooking pot with paper towels, then put it back on the heat. Pour in the wine and deglaze the pot, scraping up the meat residues from the bottom of the pot. Pour in half of the chicken bouillon. Return all the ingredients to the pot and pour in most of the remaining bouillon (reserve a scant ¼cup/50 ml for warming the rabbit just before serving). Simmer for 1 hour 30 minutes. Strain the gravy through a fine mesh sieve.

■

Prepare the vegetables. Cook the green beans in boiling water for 5 minutes, then drain them and immerse them immediately in iced water to stop the cooking. Drain them again and place them on paper towels to dry them well. Repeat this process to cook the pea pods (2 minutes), peas (3 minutes) and fava beans (1 minute). Once the fava beans are cool, peel them. Mix the vegetables together.

Cook the macaroni until al dente in a large volume of salted boiling water. Keep warm.

In a skillet, brown the marinated rabbit legs in the remaining 2 tablespoons of olive oil. Cook them for just 2 minutes on each side to keep the flesh pink. Lay the legs in a dish, cover with foil, and leave the meat to rest.

Deglaze the pan with the gravy, reduce, then add the Meaux and Dijon mustards. Season with salt and pepper. When the gravy is thick enough to coat the back of a spoon, stir in the sherry vinegar. Keep the gravy warm.

Place the rabbit legs in the pan with the reserved bouillon and warm through. Divide the macaroni among soup plates and arrange the rabbit and vegetables on top. Pour over plenty of gravy and serve immediately.

Enjoy with a Chablis Fourchaume "Domaine Charly Nicolle" 2016.

A FAMILY RITUAL

At lunchtime, La Fontaine de Mars is also a family restaurant, with which generations of regulars have formed close ties over the years. People who came here as children return as parents, and then as grandparents. It's a place where families meet up, especially for Sunday lunch. Indeed, the restaurant's table plan varies very little from one Sunday to the next: for the loyal customers who have been coming here all, or most, of their lives, you could say that La Fontaine de Mars is part of the family.

It's no wonder, then, that some arrange to hold festive dinners here. Or that they choose to make it the setting for a happy event, like the young man who wanted to trace a path of candles to the restaurant's terrace to welcome his girlfriend before formally asking for her hand in marriage. Or another man in love who had the idea of getting the restaurant staff to bury the engagement ring at the bottom of a glass of strawberry zabaglione and then asking his sweetheart to marry him over dessert. Whether the occasion is large or small, La Fontaine de Mars has been a constant witness to families growing, generations succeeding each other, and life taking its course.

A CERTAIN MR SMITH

Among the restaurant's fine customers are personalities whose names are as daunting as they are famous. And sometimes, behind the celebrity mask, one discovers the most sympathetic of individuals. One winter day, a major Parisian hotel called the restaurant to reserve a table for a certain Mr Smith. Early that evening, Christiane Boudon was informed that Mr Smith had arrived at the restaurant. She went outside to meet the gentleman, who was wearing a cap pulled down to his eyes, and greeted him—"Bonjour, monsieur Smith"—without having the least idea of who was hiding behind this ubiquitous surname. The complicity was immediate with this discreet man—who turned out to be none other than Robert De Niro. Since that first time, the American star has been welcomed as a friend at La Fontaine de Mars. A great lover of foie gras and chicken with morel mushrooms, which he usually accompanies with a good white wine, the actor is the most affable of diners, who, once he has been fed, will happily chat to the serving staff as would any regular customer, and never forgets to congratulate the chef on his skills.

FREE-RANGE CHICKEN SUPREMES
WITH MOREL MUSHROOMS AND PILAF RICE

SERVES 6
·

PREP: 40 MINUTES
COOK: 1 HOUR
·

Ingredients

FOR THE MOREL SAUCE:
1 ¾ lb. (800 g) medium morel mushrooms
½ cup (2 ¾ oz./80 g) finely chopped shallots
3 ½ tablespoons (1 ¾ oz./50 g) butter
Scant ¼ cup (50 ml) Monbazillac or vin jaune
2 cups (500 ml) veal bouillon

3 ⅓ cups (800 ml) whipping cream
Salt and pepper

FOR PILAF RICE:
½ onion
½ shallot
2 tablespoons (30 g) butter
1 teaspoon olive oil
2 cups (14 oz./400 g) US rice
3 cups (700 ml) chicken bouillon
1 bouquet garni

3 ½ tablespoons (1 ¾ oz./50 g) butter

FOR THE SUPREMES:
6 free-range chicken cutlets
1 teaspoon olive oil
3 ½ tablespoons (1 ¾ oz./50 g) butter

Make the morel sauce. Thoroughly wash the morels by soaking them for a few minutes in cold water. You can add a dash of white vinegar to remove any impurities and insects from the spores of the mushrooms. Repeat the process three times then drain the morels.

Sauté the shallots in a pan with the butter until soft but not colored. Add the morels and cook for a few minutes over very low heat until soft. Pour in the Monbazillac (or vin jaune, for more bitterness), stir, then add the veal bouillon. Simmer gently for 5 minutes. Stir in the cream and continue cooking over low heat for 10 minutes. Season with salt and pepper. Keep the morel sauce warm.

Make the pilaf rice. Preheat the oven to 325°F (160°C). Finely chop the onion and shallot. In a casserole, sauté them for a few minutes in the butter and oil without coloring. Add the rice and stir until transparent. Pour in the chicken bouillon and add the bouquet garni. Bring to a boil and cook, covered for 19 minutes, until the rice has absorbed all the liquid. Season with salt and pepper. Stir in the butter.

Make the supremes. Preheat the oven to 360°F (180°C). In another casserole, brown the chicken cutlets, skin side down, in the oil. Once the skin has turned golden, turn the cutlets over and baste the flesh with butter. Season with salt and pepper. Cook in the oven for 12 minutes, leaving the cutlets skin side down to keep them tender.

Arrange the chicken supremes on warm plates. Add a small dome of pilaf rice and coat generously with the morel sauce.

Enjoy with a young Côte-Rôtie "La Barbarine" 2015 by Yves Gangloff.

■

A PLACE FOR REUNIONS

■

A joyful and relaxed atmosphere greets everyone who crosses the threshold. Between bistro and brasserie, La Fontaine de Mars is a place of constantly renewed reunions with family and friends, and also, for those who are only passing through, a place that conveys the very essence of Paris.

It's a place to come and share a seafood platter, a terrine or a blanquette, to laugh and to raise a toast together. The ambiance of La Fontaine de Mars is what it is because conviviality is in the restaurant's very DNA. In the same way, the sense of hospitality is integral to Christiane Boudon, who devotes herself wholeheartedly to greeting her cherished guests, wonderfully assisted by her teams, who lavish special attention on each diner.

Well placed as they are to understand that such timeless moments spent with loved ones around a table create wonderful memories, the Boudons, too, like to take the opportunity to gather with their close friends and children here. They take pleasure in extended moments of friendship and sharing, becoming, in their turn, carefree and contented guests.

IT'S A PLACE TO COME AND SHARE A SEAFOOD PLATTER, A TERRINE OR A BLANQUETTE, TO LAUGH AND TO RAISE A TOAST TOGETHER. THE AMBIANCE OF LA FONTAINE DE MARS IS WHAT IT IS BECAUSE CONVIVIALITY IS IN THE RESTAURANT'S VERY DNA.

BETWEEN BISTRO AND BRASSERIE,
LA FONTAINE DE MARS IS A PLACE OF
CONSTANTLY RENEWED REUNIONS
WITH FAMILY AND FRIENDS, AND ALSO,
FOR THOSE WHO ARE ONLY PASSING
THROUGH, A PLACE THAT CONVEYS
THE VERY ESSENCE OF PARIS.

WELL PLACED AS THEY ARE
TO UNDERSTAND THAT SUCH
TIMELESS MOMENTS SPENT
WITH LOVED ONES AROUND
A TABLE CREATE WONDERFUL
MEMORIES, THE BOUDONS,
TOO, LIKE TO TAKE
THE OPPORTUNITY TO GATHER
WITH THEIR CLOSE FRIENDS
AND CHILDREN HERE.

BLANQUETTE DE VEAU
A THURSDAY TRADITION

SERVES 6

•

PREP: 40 MINUTES
COOK: 2 HOUR 30 MINUTES

•

Ingredients

FOR THE BLANQUETTE
1 lb. 5 oz. (600 g) veal blade, diced
1 lb. 5 oz. (600 g) veal shoulder, diced
1 onion
2 cloves
1 carrot
1 ¾ oz. (50 g) white mushrooms
1 bouquet garni
1 ¼ cups (300 ml) whipping cream

1 egg yolk
1 tablespoon thick crème fraîche
1 tablespoon lemon juice
Salt and pepper

FOR THE ROUX
3 ½ tablespoons (1 ¾ oz./50 g) butter
Generous 1/3 cup (1 ¾ oz./50 g) all-purpose flour

FOR THE GLAZED MUSHROOMS
Scant ¼ cup (50 ml) water
Pinch of sugar
2 tablespoons (30 g) butter

1 tablespoon lemon juice
7 oz. (200 g) button mushrooms

FOR THE GLAZED ONIONS:
Scant ¼ cup (50 ml) water
Pinch of sugar
2 tablespoons (30 g) butter
7 oz. (200 g) pearl onions

FOR THE PILAF RICE
(see recipe on page 72)

Make the blanquette. In a cooking pot, blanch the veal blade and shoulder by covering the meat with cold water, then bringing it to a boil and skimming off impurities. Add the onion studded with the cloves, the carrot, white mushrooms, and the bouquet garni. Season with salt and pepper. Simmer for 1 hour 30 minutes, until the meat is perfectly tender. Remove the meat from the pot and set aside. Discard the vegetables and bouquet garni and reserve the bouillon.

Make the roux. In a saucepan, melt the butter without coloring it and add the flour. Stir and simmer over very low heat for 20 minutes to obtain a very white roux.

Stir the roux into the bouillon in the cooking pot and let it simmer for 15 minutes. Add salt and pepper. Finish by stirring in the whipping cream.

Prepare the mushrooms. In a small saucepan, heat the water, sugar, butter, and lemon juice. Season with salt and pepper. Add the mushrooms and cook, without coloring, until all the liquid has evaporated. Prepare the onions in the same way (but you won't need to add lemon juice).

Put the meat, mushrooms, and onions into the pot with the creamy sauce. Heat without boiling.

In a bowl, mix the egg yolk and the thick crème fraîche, then stir in the lemon juice. Gently stir this mixture into the blanquette. From this point on, the blanquette must not be allowed to boil or it risks curdling.

To serve, arrange some pieces of veal on warm plates, add some mushrooms and glazed onions, and pour over the sauce. Serve with the pilaf rice.

Enjoy with a Crozes Hermitage Blanc 2015 by Yann Chave.

"MAURICE, A MISCHIEVOUS MAN IN HIS SEVENTIES, IS OUR WINTER MASCOT. HE CAN HOLD FORTH FOR HOURS ON THE VIRTUES OF EACH OYSTER AND CAN OPEN THEM, WITH THE SKILL OF A GOLDSMITH, AT INCREDIBLE SPEED. HE HAS HIS OWN FAN CLUB AMONG THE RESTAURANT'S CLIENTELE AS WELL AS WITH THE NEIGHBORS. WHEN WE CLOSE THE OYSTER BAR TO MAKE WAY FOR THE SUMMER TERRACE, WE'RE HEAVY-HEARTED AT THE THOUGHT OF NOT HEARING HIS CHATTER, BUT WE KNOW THAT, COME NOVEMBER 1, HE'LL BE BACK WITH US AGAIN."

CHRISTIANE BOUDON

CRAB "FONDANT"
WITH TOMATO JELLY AND AVOCADO

SERVES 6
■
PREP:
1 HOUR 30 MINUTES
REST:
14 HOURS
COOK:
1 HOUR 45 MINUTES
■

Ingredients

FOR THE CRAB FILLING:
1 orange
1 lemon
3 quarts (2.8 l) water
2 cups (500 ml) white wine
2 carrots
1 onion, cut in half
3 juniper berries
1 bouquet garni
2 live crabs (about 1 ¾ lb./800 g)
1 zucchini

5 oz. (150 g) celery root
½ tablespoon olive oil
2 cups (500 ml) whipping cream
3 thyme sprigs
A few chives, chopped
Coarse salt and pepper

FOR THE TOMATO JELLY:
2 sheets of gelatin
1 scant cup (200 ml) organic
tomato juice

The day before, make the crab filling. Make cuts in the skin of the orange and lemon (to allow the citrus aroma to diffuse) and place the fruits into a large pan. Pour in the water and the white wine and add the carrot, onion, juniper berries, bouquet garni and a pinch each of coarse salt and pepper. Boil this nage for 45 minutes, then plunge the crabs into it. As soon as the liquid returns to a boil, turn off the heat and leave the crabs in the pan until the nage has cooled. Remove the crabs with a slotted spoon and place them in the fridge. Cooking them the day before gives the crabs time to drain thoroughly and makes them easier to shell.

The next day, shell the crabs to remove all the flesh (be careful that no very thin bits of shell get into the crabmeat).

Finely dice the carrot, zucchini, and celery root, then sauté them quickly in the olive oil—they should remain crunchy.

In a saucepan, heat the cream with the thyme sprigs until fairly thick. Turn off the heat, remove the thyme, strain the cream through a fine mesh sieve, and leave to cool.

Recipe continues, following page

FOR THE CRUSHED AVOCADO:
2 avocados
½ tablespoon lemon juice
½ bunch of cilantro
Pinch of Espelette pepper

Gently mix the crabmeat with the vegetables and the thyme cream to combine, then stir in the chopped chives. Season with salt and pepper. Set the crab filling aside in the fridge.

Make the tomato jelly. Soften the gelatin sheets in a bowl of cold water for 3 minutes. In a saucepan, heat the tomato juice and add the well-drained gelatin leaves. Season with salt and pepper. Leave to cool. The tomato jelly will be poured over the crab mixture when it is practically cold and fairly thick (to check the consistency, dip a wooden spoon into it: the line should remain clean).

Prepare the crushed avocado. In a small bowl, crush the avocado flesh roughly with the lemon juice. Stir in the chopped cilantro and Espelette pepper. Season to taste with salt. Set aside in the fridge.

Place a ½-inch (1-cm) layer of the crushed avocado in each of six individual circles and press down well. Then fill with the crab mixture to ¼ inch (0.5 cm) from the top of the circle. Finish with a ¼-inch (0.5-cm) layer of tomato jelly. Refrigerate for 2 hours.

Carefully unmold the crab "fondants" onto the middle of the plates and serve with sourdough toast.

Enjoy with a Pouilly Fumé "Château de Tracy" 2017
by the Comtesse d'Estutt d'Assay.

PANFRIED BABY CUTTLEFISH

Ingredients

3 ¼ lb. (1.5 kg) baby cuttlefish
1 tablespoon olive oil
1 tablespoon lemon juice

FOR THE MASHED POTATO:
1 ¾ lb. (800 g) Ratte potatoes
2 teaspoons milk
Scant ¼ cup (50 ml) whipping cream
²/₃ cup (5 oz./150 g) butter, diced

FOR THE CRUSHED TOMATOES:
3 tomatoes
1 shallot
1 cup (5 oz./150 g) pitted black olives
1 ¼ cups (300 ml)
Pinch of Espelette pepper
A few basil leaves
A few chives

SERVES 6

∎

PRÉPARATION : 1 H 30
CUISSON : 40 MIN

∎

To prepare the baby cuttlefish, start by separating the body from the head. Cut the bodies in half, empty them, and scrape to remove the entrails. Remove the "beaks" from the heads by pressing at the level of the tentacles, being careful not to puncture the ink sac. Rinse the baby cuttlefish, drain them, and dry them in a clean kitchen towel.

Make the mashed potato. Peel the potatoes, cut them in half, and steam them for about 25 minutes. Mash them by hand (don't use a food processor or stick blender or the puree may become gluey). In a saucepan, heat the milk and cream, then pour into the mashed potato. Stir in the butter and stir everything until smooth and even. Keep it warm.

Prepare the crushed tomatoes. Quarter the tomatoes, remove the core and seeds, and cut the flesh into strips. Finely chop

the shallot and roughly chop the olives. In a bowl, toss together the tomatoes, shallot, and olives, then stir in the 1 ¼ cups (300 ml) olive oil, Espelette pepper, and chopped basil and chives.

Heat the 1 tablespoon of olive oil in a skillet and, when it is beginning to smoke, toss in a few baby cuttlefish. As soon as they shrink and begin to color, add two tablespoons of the crushed tomatoes. Stir, then remove from the heat and keep warm. By cooking the cuttlefish in stages like this, you prevent the sauce from boiling, which could make the cuttlefish tough. Deglaze the pan with the lemon juice to make a sauce.

To serve, place two large spoons of mashed potato on each warm plate and top them with the panfried baby cuttlefish. Drizzle with a little sauce and serve immediately.

Enjoy with a Rosé Corse de Figari "Clos Canarelli" 2018.

SALT-CRUSTED BASS

Ingredients

FOR THE BASS:
3 line-caught bass (each
about 2 ¼ lb./1 kg)
3 thyme sprigs
1 bunch of flat-leaf parsley
1 fennel bulb, including
fronds

FOR THE SALT CRUST:
1 cup (8 ¾ oz./250 g)
Guérande coarse sea salt
4 cups (1 lb. 2 oz./500 g)
all-purpose flour
Scant ¼ cup (50 ml)
white wine
Scant ¼ cup (50 ml)
white vinegar
3 thyme sprigs,
leaves crushed
1 cup (250 ml) water
1 egg yolk beaten with
1 tablespoon water

FOR THE RELISH:
1 tomato
½ preserved lemon
¾ cup (4 ¼ oz./120 g)
pitted black olives
½ bunch of chives
1 shallot
1 scant cup (200 ml)
olive oil

FOR THE MASHED POTATO
(see recipe on page 94)

SERVES 6

■

PREP: 30 MINUTES
COOK: 25 MINUTES

■

Prepare the bass. Select some good line-caught bass from your fishmonger, ensuring that you consume this fish only between June and February, outside of its spawning season. Ask your fishmonger to gut them by making an incision of about 2 inches (5 cm) in the belly. Peel and quarter the fennel and chop the fronds. Stuff each bass with a sprig each of thyme and parsley, a fennel quarter, and some of the fronds. Set aside in the fridge.

Prepare the salt crust. In a bowl, combine the coarse sea salt, flour, white wine, vinegar, crushed thyme leaves, and water to obtain a firm paste. Roll the dough out to a thickness of ¼ inch (5 mm). Set aside in the fridge.

Preheat the oven to 350°C (170°C). Wrap each bass in the dough, forming it into a fish shape and brush the top with the beaten egg yolk, using a pastry brush. Place the bass on a baking sheet and bake for 25 minutes.

Make the relish. Finely dice the tomato, preserved lemon, and olives. Finely chop the shallot. Mix together in a bowl and stir in the chives and olive oil.

Remove the fish from the oven and immediately break the salt crust and open it out. Lift the bass fillets, taking care to remove all small bones, and serve on warm plates with a quenelle of mashed potato. Serve the relish separately.

Enjoy with a Côtes-de-Provence blanc "Château de Selle" 2016 from Domaines d'Ott.

COD LOIN
WITH AIOLI

SERVES 6

PREP:
1 HOUR 30 MINUTES
COOK: 1 HOUR

Ingredients

FOR THE AIOLI:
2 ¼ oz. (60 g) firm-fleshed potato
Scant 1½ cup (100 ml) fish stock
2 saffron threads
4½ oz. (12g) Lautrec pink garlic cloves (about 3 cloves)

¾ tablespoon Dijon mustard
1 scant cup (200 ml) olive oil
Salt and pepper

FOR THE COD:
6 cod loin fillets (each about 5 ¾ oz./160 g), skin and small bones removed
Scant ¼ cup (1 ¾ oz./50 g) coarse salt
Olive oil

FOR THE BABY VEGETABLES:
2 Roseval potatoes
3 baby turnips
3 baby carrots
3 baby onions
5 oz. (150 g) pea pods (about 2 cups)
5 oz. (150 g) green beans (about 1 ½ cups cut into 1-inch/2.5-cm lengths)
Freshly ground pepper

Make the aioli. Peel the potatoes and cut each into six pieces. Pour the fish stock into a saucepan, add the potatoes and saffron, and cook until all the liquid has evaporated. Season with salt and pepper. Crush the potatoes with a pestle.

Hard-boil the 4 eggs for 8 minutes in boiling water. Cool them under cold running water, then peel them. Remove the germ from the garlic then crush. Place it in a bowl with the raw egg yolk, 1 hard-boiled egg yolk, and the mustard. Gradually whisk in the olive oil then add the mashed potato, a little at a time. Set aside the aioli in the fridge.

Prepare the cod. Cover the cod with the coarse salt and leave for 10 minutes to firm the flesh and prevent it from crumbling when cooked. Rinse the fish and dry carefully with paper towels. Set aside in the fridge.

Prepare the baby vegetables. Peel the vegetables, cut the larger ones into two or three pieces, then cook the different vegetables separately for a few minutes in salted water to keep them crisp. Refresh them immediately in iced water, then drain them. Keep warm.

Steam the cod loin fillets for 4 minutes, until they have a pearly sheen—you should be able to see a little "rainbow" on the white flesh.

Arrange the baby vegetables on the plates, place half a hard-boiled egg on top, and add a grind of pepper. Place a cod loin fillet next to the vegetables and drizzle over some olive oil. Serve the aioli separately.

Enjoy with a white Macon Cruzille "les Perrières" 2016 by the Guillot-Broux Family.

TIME TO EXPAND

In the 2000s, La Fontaine de Mars was operating perfectly as a Parisian bistro. When the two small shops next to the restaurant were put up for sale in 2005 and 2006 respectively, Jacques and Christiane Boudon seized the unexpected opportunity to expand the scale of their business.

The issue of interior decoration was settled from the outset: the style of La Fontaine de Mars needed to remain the same or it would lose its soul. The couple relied on the talent of their decorator, Christian Maitre a specialist in Parisian brasseries, to enlarge the premises and seamlessly merge the old and new spaces. The gamble paid off: the authenticity of the place was scrupulously preserved. And when the expanded premises were opened on May 9, 2007, nothing seemed to have changed at La Fontaine de Mars except the size of the place. The mirrors, radiators, and all the carefully crafted furniture blended into the restaurant as if they had been quietly aging there for decades. In this familiar atmosphere, loyal customers returned to their routines in an instant.

A real transformation had nevertheless taken place. More spacious, the old bistro had become the elegant traditional brasserie that Jacques and Christiane Boudon had always dreamed of. The restaurant had been given a new lease of life. With a larger and better equipped kitchen, and an expanded team, the chef could now fulfil his potential. La Fontaine de Mars had gained standing.

AN ILLUSTRIOUS VISIT

June 6, 2009 will remain a special date in the history of La Fontaine de Mars. That morning, Christiane Boudon had flown to New York for a promotion. Meanwhile, there was the usual Saturday buzz in the restaurant, which was full for both services. It just so happened that the US Embassy had reserved the top room for dinner. That was no big surprise: the ambassador was a regular diner.

At 5 p.m., members of the embassy security service asked to speak to Jacques Boudon. They wanted to visit the restaurant, then the building and its surroundings. This was not the usual procedure. What was going on? It took Jacques a few seconds to understand what he was being told with such secrecy. It wasn't the ambassador who would be dining there tonight, but the US President himself!

Barack Obama, who had been elected to office a few months previously, would be going to Normandy for D-Day commemorations before spending the night in Paris, and he wished to have dinner with his family and some friends at La Fontaine de Mars.

While Jacques was still stunned by the news, everything was nevertheless getting into motion around him. Measures appropriate to the importance of the event were set in place. US protocol officials and the security service took control. The first instruction was simple: do not talk about this exceptional visit to anyone or the event will be canceled. It was to be a top-secret private dinner. Then, two restaurant employees who spoke English fluently were appointed to serve Obama and his guests.

WHEN THINGS GET BUSY AND IT'S ALL HANDS ON DECK, THE TEAM TAKES TO THE FLOOR WITH A CERTAIN EXCITEMENT AND THE SENSE THAT THEY HAVE A LOT TO LIVE UP TO— A BIT LIKE IN THE THEATER, WHERE, NIGHT AFTER NIGHT, EACH PERFORMANCE IS LIKE THE FIRST TIME.

CLASSIC CARAMEL CREAM
WITH LANGUES DE CHAT COOKIES

SERVES 6

■

PREP: 15 MINUTES
REST: 45 MINUTES
COOK:
1 HOUR 10 MINUTES

■

Ingredients

FOR THE LANGUES DE CHAT:
1 egg white, beaten
½ tablespoon all-purpose flour
½ tablespoon confectioners' sugar
4 teaspoons melted butter

FOR THE CARAMEL:
²/₃ cup (4 ½ oz./125 g)
superfine sugar
1 tablespoon water

FOR THE CREAM:
1 Bourbon vanilla bean
5 whole eggs + 8 yolks
²/₃ cup (4 ½ oz./125 g)
superfine sugar
2 cups (500 ml) whole milk
2 cups (500 ml) whipping cream

Make the langues de chat. In a bowl, whisk the egg white with the sifted flour and confectioners' sugar until the mixture whitens. Stir in the melted butter then let the dough rest for 45 minutes. Preheat the oven to 360°F (180°C). Place small spoons of dough on a non-stick baking sheet, giving the cookies a slightly elongated shape, and bake for 4 minutes.

Make the caramel. In a saucepan, heat the sugar and water until lightly caramelized. Stop the cooking by dipping the bottom of the pan in a little water. Pour the caramel into six ramekins, tilting them to ensure that the caramel coats the bottom and sides of each ramekin. Let the caramel cool.

Make the cream. Preheat the oven to 200°F (90°C). Split the vanilla bean lengthwise and scrape out the seeds. In a bowl, whisk the whole eggs and the yolks with the sugar and half the vanilla seeds. In a saucepan, heat the milk and cream with the remaining vanilla seeds and half the bean. Let cool, remove the vanilla bean, pour over the egg mixture, and stir in. Pour the creamy mixture into the caramel-coated ramekins, without creating a mousse. Place the ramekins in a bain-marie and bake in the oven for 40 minutes. Leave to cool completely then turn the crèmes caramel out onto cold plates. The caramel will then coat the dessert. Serve with the langues de chat cookies.

Enjoy with a Sauternes "Château de Fargues" 2007 by Count Lur Saluces.

GUILLAUME'S SUNDAY TARTE TATIN

SERVES 6

·

PREP: 30 MINUTES
REST: 30 MINUTES
COOK: 55 MINUTES

·

Ingredients

14 oz. (400 g) puff pastry from your baker
15 Golden Delicious apples
1 cup + 2 tablespoons (8 oz./225 g) superfine sugar
½ cup (4 ¼ oz./120 g) butter
Isigny crème fraiche, to serve

Roll out the puff pastry into a circle a little larger than your round baking pan. Peel, core, and halve the apples. Set aside. Preheat the oven to 350°C (170°C).

In a saucepan, heat the sugar and butter until lightly caramelized, then pour this caramel into the pan, set over heat. Remove from the heat and pack the apples, upright, into the pan. Fill any gaps with small pieces of apple.

Bake for 30 minutes, then remove the pan from the oven and check that the apples are soft. Place the pan on a very low heat to evaporate the cooking juices from the apples. With a spatula, carefully straighten up the apples.

Cover with the puff pastry, pressing down around the edge of the pan to ensure that all the apples are well covered. Return the pan to the oven and bake for an additional 16 minutes. Leave to cool for 30 minutes then firmly but carefully turn the tarte Tatin out onto a serving plate.

Serve the tarte Tatin still warm with crème fraîche.

Enjoy with a well-chilled "Argelette" cider by Éric Bordelet.

TARTE BOURDALOUE

SERVES 6

•

PREP: 45 MINUTES
REST: 30 HOURS
COOK: 1 HOUR 35 MINUTES

•

Ingredients

FOR THE SWEET PIE DOUGH:
2 cups (8 ¾ oz./250 g)
all-purpose flour
Pinch of salt
3 egg yolks
½ cup (3 ½ oz./100 g)
superfine sugar
1 tablespoon cold water
Generous ½ cup (4 ½ oz./
125 g) softened butter

FOR THE POACHED PEARS:
4 pears
8 cups (2 l) water
2 ½ cups (1 lb. 2 oz./
500 g) superfine sugar
1 cinnamon stick
1 orange
1 lemon

FOR THE ALMOND CREAM:
3 eggs
⅔ cup (4 ½ oz./125 g)
superfine sugar
1 ¼ cups (4 ½ oz./125 g)
ground almonds
½ cup + 2 teaspoons
(4 ½ oz./125 g) melted
butter
2 tablespoons pear brandy

The day before, make the sweet pie dough. Place the flour, salt, egg yolks, sugar, and cold water in a food-processor bowl and pulse until the dough forms a ball. Add the butter, cut into small pieces. Put the dough in a bowl, cover with a clean kitchen towel and refrigerate for 24 hours.

The next day, remove the dough from the fridge and leave to stand for 20 minutes before rolling it out to a thickness of ½ inch (1 cm). Use the dough to line a pie plate, leaving a thick rim, and refrigerate for 3 hours.

Preheat the oven to 350°C (170°C). Cover the bottom of the pie plate with foil and fill with pie weights. Bake for 15 minutes, then remove the foil and pie weights and bake for a further 5 minutes. Allow the pie shell to cool.

Poach the pears. Peel the pears and remove the seeds using an apple corer. In a saucepan, heat the water and sugar, then add the cinnamon stick, orange, and lemon. Leave the fruits whole but score the peel so that their aromas are diffused in the syrup. When the syrup begins to boil, add the pears and leave them to poach for 30 minutes. Place a clean kitchen towel over the pan to totally immerse the fruits and prevent them rising to the surface: this will ensure that the pears cook evenly and that their flesh remains very white. Drain the pears, cut them in half, and place them to drain for 2 hours on paper towels to prevent them releasing too much juice into the tart.

Make the almond cream. Preheat the oven to 325°F (160°C). In a bowl, whisk the eggs and sugar, then add the ground almonds, melted butter, and pear brandy. Set aside.

Arrange the pear halves in the pie shell, cut side down, and pour over the almond cream without completely covering the pears. Bake for 45 minutes, until the pie is nicely golden. Remove from the oven and let stand for 1 hour, then serve generous slices, with some pear sorbet, perhaps.

Enjoy with "Poiré Authentique" by Éric Bordelet.

MERINGUE
WITH BERRIES

SERVES 6

PREP: 45 MINUTES
COOK: 1 HOUR 40 MINUTES

Ingredients

FOR THE MERINGUE:
2 ¾ oz. (80 g) egg white
(about 2 large whites)
⅓ cup (2 1/4 oz./65 g)
superfine sugar
½ cup unsifted (2 ¼ oz./65 g)
confectioners' sugar

FOR CRÈME PÂTISSIÈRE:
2 cups (500 ml) milk
1 Bourbon vanilla bean
5 egg yolks

Scant ½ cup (3 ¼ oz./90 g)
superfine sugar
½ cup (2 ½ oz./70 g) all-purpose flour
½ teaspoon confectioners' sugar
1 cup (250 ml) whipping cream

1 lb. 2 oz. (500 g) Mara des Bois
strawberries
A few blueberries, raspberries,
and red currants
Red-berry coulis

Make the meringue. Preheat the oven to 315°C (155°C). Whisk the egg whites until stiff, then whisk in first the superfine sugar and then the confectioners' sugar. Keep whisking. Carefully spoon the meringue into a piping bag fitted with a plain tip and pipe six disks on a silicone mat. Bake in the oven for 1 hour 20 minutes. Leave to cool.

Make the crème pâtissière. In a saucepan, heat the milk with the split and scraped vanilla bean. In a bowl, whisk the egg yolks with the superfine sugar until they turn white, then sift in the flour and combine. Pour in a ladle of hot milk to thin the mixture, then pour it into the pan. Cook without stirring for 10 minutes. Leave the crème pâtissière to cool, stirring it regularly to prevent a skin forming on top. Set aside in the fridge.

Quickly rinse the raspberries, strawberries, and blueberries under cold water, then drain them. Cut the strawberries into two or three pieces.

Spread a circle of chilled crème pâtissière on each plate, scatter over the berries, and top with a meringue. Serve with red-berry coulis.

Enjoy with a Pol Roger "Cuvée Pure" Extra Brut Champagne.

STRAWBERRIES
WITH VANILLA AND PISTACHIO ZABAGLIONE

Ingredients

1 lb. 10 oz. (750 g) Mara des Bois
strawberries
8 ¾ oz. (250 g) wild strawberries

FOR THE ZABAGLIONE
5 egg yolks
5 tablespoons superfine sugar
5 tablespoons Monbazillac
2 teaspoons pistachio paste
1 cup (250 ml) whipping cream
6 scoops (500 ml) vanilla ice cream
1 scant cup (200 ml) red-berry coulis
⅓ cup (1 ¾ oz./50 g) shelled unsalted
pistachios, toasted

SERVES 6

∎

PREP: 25 MINUTES
COOK: 10 MINUTES

∎

Carefully wash, hull, and dry the strawberries.

Make the zabaglione. In a bowl, whisk the egg yolks, sugar, and Monbazillac until the mixture is frothy. Stir in the pistachio paste. Place the bowl in a bain-marie and heat until it reaches a temperature of 140°F (60°C). Remove from the heat and whisk the zabaglione until completely cool.

In another bowl, whip the cream, then gently fold it into the zabaglione. Set aside in the fridge.

Place a scoop of vanilla ice cream at the bottom of each glass, divide the strawberries among the glasses, then pour over the red-berry coulis. Finally, add two spoons of zabaglione and top with the toasted pistachios.

Enjoy with well-chilled Billecart-Salmon Pink Champagne.

GRIOTTINE CLAFOUTIS

SERVES 6

·

PREP: 20 MINUTES
COOK: 35 MINUTES

·

Ingredients

²/₃ cup (5 oz./150 g) butter
+ 1–2 tablespoons for the molds
2 whole eggs + 4 yolks
¾ cup (5 oz./150 g) superfine sugar
+ ¼ cup (1 ¾ oz./50 g) for the molds
1 ¼ cups (5 oz./150 g) all-purpose flour
+ ¹/₃ cup (5 oz./150 g) for the molds
1 ½ cups (375 ml) milk
48 griottines
2 cups (500 ml) vanilla ice cream

In a saucepan, melt the butter until it turns light brown in color and releases a nutty aroma (*beurre noisette*). Leave to cool.

In a bowl, whisk the eggs and egg yolks with the sugar until the mixture whitens. Whisk in the flour, then the milk and the *beurre noisette*.

Preheat the oven to 325°F (160°C). Drain the griottines. Butter, flour, and sugar six individual molds, then place 8 griottines in each. Carefully pour the mixture into the molds, leaving ½ an inch (1 cm) at the top, and bake in the oven for 30 minutes.

Serve the griottine clafoutis warm with a quenelle of vanilla ice cream.

Enjoy with a glass of Guignolet Kirsch from the Peureux distillery.

MONT BLANC

Ingredients

FOR THE LITTLE MERINGUES:
2 ¾ oz. (80 g) egg white
(about 2 large whites)
⅓ cup (2 ¼ oz./65 g)
superfine sugar
½ cup unsifted (2 ¼ oz./65 g)
confectioners' sugar

FOR THE COCOA SAUCE:
⅝ cup (150 ml) water
½ cup (1 ¾ oz./50 g) bitter cocoa powder
¼ cup unsifted (1 oz./30 g)
confectioners' sugar

FOR THE MONT BLANCS:
2 cups (500 ml) whipping cream
5 oz. (150 g) sweetened chestnut puree
6 marrons glacés in syrup

SERVES 6

∎

PREP: 15 MINUTES
COOK: 2 HOURS 35 MINUTES

∎

Make the little meringues. Preheat the oven to 300°F (150°C). Whisk the egg whites until stiff, then whisk in first the superfine sugar and then the confectioners' sugar. Keep whisking. Carefully spoon the meringue into a piping bag fitted with a plain tip and pipe six small balls of meringue on a silicone mat. Bake in the oven for 2 hours 30 minutes.

Make the cocoa sauce. In a saucepan, heat the water, cocoa, and confectioners' sugar to boiling point, while stirring to obtain a smooth consistency. Leave the cocoa sauce to cool down.

Make the Mont Blanc. Whip the cream then spoon it gently into a piping bag fitted with a large star tip. Whip the chestnut puree to soften it and place a layer in the bottom of six glasses. Place a small meringue and a marron glacé on top. Pipe a dome of whipped cream, drizzle with a little cocoa sauce, and serve immediately.

Enjoy with a late-harvest Gewurztraminer "Fronholz" 2009
by André Ostertag.

The neighborhood was soon completely cordoned off by the police and the bakery opposite the restaurant was requisitioned as a command post.

During the late afternoon, security measures were further intensified. An ambulance was parked in front of the establishment, a convoy of security cars was stationed around the area, and the street was closed to traffic and pedestrians. The stage was set.

7 P.M. Restaurant staff, posted at the various accesses to the street, were instructed to filter guests with a reservation for the evening.

7.30 P.M. As the service began in the downstairs room, there was feverish excitement in the air. Sensing that something unusual was going on, the guests were not completely focused on their meals. You could have heard a pin drop.

8.30 P.M. Still nobody. The tension continued to mount while the number of guests announced by the Embassy was constantly varying. There would be nine, then eight, then there was a rumor that the President was tired. Would they still come?

9 P.M. A new call set operations in motion. The presidential car, containing six people, had just left the US embassy. There was just time to lay the table again before the President arrived, accompanied by his wife Michelle and his friends. From their windows, local residents were cheering the statesman like a rock star.

Barack Obama greeted Jacques Boudon with a friendly handshake and then moved upstairs with his guests. Jacques was asked to remain in the adjoining room with the protocol officials. The delegation included no less than a hundred people, including bodyguards on the alert. Immersed in a frenzy the like of which they had never experienced, the restaurant staff felt as though they were in a movie.

Around the table, everything was going swimmingly. The President and his guests were obviously appreciating the dishes and the atmosphere was very relaxed. So much so that at the end of the meal, Barak Obama accepted the after-dinner liqueur offered by Jacques Boudon, extending his visit by a good half hour beyond the time that had been allocated by protocol officials. The statesman finally left the restaurant after having warmly thanked Boudon and the whole team for the excellent time he spent in his fine brasserie.

The evening had been a great success, but it was not yet time to relax. The security teams demanded that the dining room be cleared as quickly as possible so as to leave no trace of what the President had eaten or drunk. Everything had to go, even the tables and chairs! When the American teams finally left the place, there was a riot. Journalists and curious visitors invaded the establishment like a wild horde and rushed to the first floor to photograph what remained of the illustrious diner's visit. They were very disappointed.

Then the second act began. From the day after the presidential visit, the restaurant's phone rang constantly, and e-mails began pouring in from all over the world to reserve Barack Obama's table. La Fontaine de Mars had become the Parisian bistro where everyone wanted to dine, to the extent that two new telephone lines had to be installed. In the kitchen, orders of œufs en meurette, foie gras, beef fillet, confit de canard and îles flottantes followed one after another: the President's "groupies" want nothing but their idol's menu.

Meanwhile, the third act was taking place in New York, where Jacques joined Christiane on June 7. While dining in a French restaurant, he had the strange feeling that he was being stared at by the other guests. It didn't take him long to understand why when people started asking him if he owned a restaurant in Paris. It was then that he discovered that his picture had been shown over and over on US TV channels during the previous 24 hours. For Americans, he had become the owner of the Parisian restaurant where their President had dined.

REVEALING THE SECRETS

behind the scenes

.

PIERRE'S FINE PALETTE

A t La Fontaine de Mars, foie gras, confit, andouillette, and cassoulet take the lead. Here, every day, the chef is committed to treating his guests to the hearty, authentic, and uncomplicated cuisine of southwestern France. And it's a task he succeeds in fabulously. He may be from Normandy rather than the South West, but he can make a cassoulet better than anyone, and his chicken with morel mushrooms has delighted celebrities from around the world. He has plenty to boast about, but the chef's not one to show off, and in any case, this is not that kind of restaurant. What motivates him more than anything is simply the desire to offer happiness by sharing his cuisine. When diners, whether famous or unknown, express their gratitude, having relished his mushroom pâté, his hare à la royale, or his divine crème brûlée, they make him the happiest of men.

This discreet and generous man is Pierre Saugrain. At dawn, he's the first to cross the threshold of La Fontaine de Mars. While he's waiting for the day's deliveries, he savors the silence of the early morning with a cup of coffee at the bar of the still-slumbering restaurant, a place he has loved for almost 30 years and that he willingly admits is his second home.

This passionate chef views cooking as a calling; he has meticulously explored (almost) every aspect of food and cooking and has honed his skills in some of the finest restaurants. He first donned the sous-chef's apron at La Fontaine de Mars on June 1, 1992, just weeks after Christiane and Jacques Boudon had taken over the reins of the place. For the first time in his life, the young man had responded to an advertisement for a job that was supposed to last for only a few months—just long enough for him to be able to enhance his CV, in fact. He had decided that working in a bistro would add to his career experience, which had already included working in several Michelin-starred restaurants. And then, much to his surprise, he fell in love with the place. He joined the restaurant as sous-chef to Eric Lefèvre, who he replaced a few years later. Spurred on by the Boudons' trust in him, the young chef quickly found his bearings and could feel his confidence growing. Constantly seeking to refine the menu, while respecting the style and spirit of the restaurant, his aim is to raise bistro cooking to its highest level. And for that, he holds all the trump cards in his hand: an expertise acquired working under Michelin-starred chefs in some top restaurants, fine produce, and an insatiable curiosity for everything related to his profession.

- Sebastian Cortès - Bayonne 1975.

h. dieuzaide

- Feria de Seville

GAME TERRINE
WITH FOIE GRAS AND FIG CHUTNEY

SERVES 6

▪

PREP: 45 MINUTES
REST: 41 HOURS
COOK: 6 HOURS

▪

Ingredients

FOR THE TERRINE:
4 shallots
3 ½ tablespoons (1 ¾ oz./50 g) butter
1 scant cup (200 ml) white wine
Pinch of superfine sugar
14 oz. (400 g) wild boar shoulder
8 ¾ oz. (250 g) blanched pork throat
1 ½ oz. (40 g) cured ham
4 oz. (115 g) pork liver
$^1/_3$ oz. (10 g) pork rind
$^1/_3$ cup (80 ml) hog's blood
½ lemon
2 tablespoons port
2 tablespoons Armagnac

Small pinch of grated nutmeg
2 juniper berries, crushed
4 oz. (115 g) raw duck foie gras
7 oz. (200 g) caul fat, soaked in a mixture
of vinegar and water
2 ½ teaspoons salt and 1 teaspoon pepper

FOR THE CHUTNEY:
2 ¼ lb. (1 kg) black figs
1 Reinette apple
1 onion, halved
½-inch (1.5-cm) piece of ginger
1 cup (7 oz./200 g) brown sugar
Pinch of ground cinnamon
1 clove
1 ½ teaspoons ground coriander
¼ teaspoon fine salt
$^5/_8$ cup (150 ml) white wine vinegar

■

The day before, make the terrine. Preheat the oven to 300°F (150°C). Peel the shallots and put them, whole, into a small pan with the butter, white wine, and sugar. Season with salt and pepper. Cook, covered, for 1 hour, until the shallots are caramelized.

Grind the wild boar shoulder, blanched pork throat, cured ham, liver, and pork rind together. Place in a bowl and mix in the caramelized shallots, blood, lemon juice, port, Armagnac, salt, pepper, grated nutmeg, and crushed juniper berries. Cover the terrine mixture with plastic wrap and refrigerate.

Cut the foie gras lengthwise and roll it in plastic wrap to form a 1 ½-inch-(4-cm) diameter sausage the length of the terrine mold. Moisten the bottom and edges of a 1-quart (1-kg) terrine mold with cold water. Drain the caul fat then use it to line the mold. Place some of the terrine mixture in the mold to halfway up the sides and press down. Carefully lay the foie gras down the middle of the mold, then cover it with the remainder of the terrine mixture. Fold the caul fat over the top of the terrine, moistening it regularly so that it's smooth. Cover with plastic wrap and refrigerate for at least 5 hours.

The next day, preheat the oven to 410°F (210°C). Cook the terrine for 5 minutes, then remove it from the oven and leave to cool for 15 minutes. Adjust the oven control to 200°F (90°C). Cook the terrine for 2–3 hours, until a probe inserted in the center registers 162°F (72°C). Leave to cool to room temperature then refrigerate. Leave the terrine in the mold for at least 36 hours before unmolding.

Make the chutney. Remove the stalk and tail from the figs, peel and seed the apple, peel the onions and ginger, then roughly chop everything. Place in a saucepan, add the brown sugar, cinnamon, clove, ground coriander, salt, and vinegar. Cook over a low heat for 2 ½ hours, stirring regularly. Leave to cool, then refrigerate.

Serve the terrine cut into thick slices, accompanied with a dollop of fig chutney and slices of country bread.

Enjoy with a red Marsannay "Domaine Trapet" 2016.

HOT FOIE GRAS
WITH CARAMELIZED PEARS

SERVES 6

■

PREP: 20 MINUTES
COOK: 1 HOUR

■

Ingredients

6 pears
3 ½ oz. (100 g) superfine sugar
Scant ¼ cup (50 ml) water
12 raw foie gras escalopes
(each about 3 oz./85 g)
1 tablespoon balsamic cream
Salt and pepper

Preheat the oven to 350°C (170°C). Peel, core, and halve the pears. In a saucepan, heat the sugar and water until lightly caramelized. Pour the caramel into a baking dish and place the pears face down on top. Cover the dish with foil and bake for about 40 minutes. Check that the pears are cooked by sticking the tip of a knife in one. Leave to cool.

Carefully score the foie gras escalopes and fry them over a high heat without fat in a non-stick skillet. Turn them over so that both sides are colored and, as soon as a crust is formed, turn the heat down to halfway. Season with salt and pepper.

Arrange the foie gras escalopes and the caramelized pears on hot plates and drizzle over a little balsamic cream.

Enjoy with a Pacherenc Vic Bilh "Vendémiaire" 2013 by Alain Brumont.

WARM PORCINI
MUSHROOM "PIE"

SERVES 6

PREP: 1 HOUR
REST: 20 MINUTES
COOK: 55 MINUTES

Ingredients

1 lb. 2 oz. (500 g) white mushrooms
2 ¼ lb. (1 kg) porcini mushrooms
1 shallot
4 teaspoons butter + 2 teaspoons for the ramekins
2 teaspoons olive oil

A few chives, chopped
A few flat-leaf parsley leaves, chopped
1 scant cup (200 ml) whipping cream
1 whole egg + 4 yolks
½ garlic clove
Salt and pepper

Peel and clean the white mushrooms, then roughly chop them. In a skillet, fry them until they release their moisture. Drain and leave to cool. Do the same with the porcini mushrooms, reserving the cooking juices.

In a skillet, sauté the chopped shallot in the butter and olive oil until soft, then add the porcini mushrooms to color them. Season with salt and pepper. At the last minute, stir in the chopped chives and parsley. Leave to cool. Finely chop (or process) the white mushrooms then mix with the porcini mushrooms.

Preheat the oven to 320°F (160°C). In a large bowl, mix together the cream, the whole egg and yolks, the mushroom cooking liquid, and the crushed garlic. Season with salt and pepper then stir in the mixed mushrooms. Butter six ramekins and fill them with the creamy mushroom mixture. Place the ramekins in a bain-marie and bake for 40 minutes. The top of the "pies" should be nicely browned. Leave to stand for 20 minutes before unmolding.

Serve these little mushroom "pies" with corn salad dressed with a truffle-oil vinaigrette and toasted country bread lightly rubbed with garlic.

Enjoy with a Corton-Charlemagne 2015 by Michel Juillot.

CALF'S HEAD SALAD
WITH ROSEVAL POTATOES

SERVES 6

PREP: 15 MINUTES
REST: 12 HOURS
COOK:
4 HOURS 30 MINUTES

Ingredients

FOR THE CALF'S HEAD:
1 lb. 5 oz. (600 g) calf's head
prepared by your butcher
1 carrot
1 onion, cut in half
1 clove
1 bouquet garni

FOR THE POTATOES:
14 oz. (400 g) Roseval potatoes
1 garlic clove

FOR THE RAVIGOTE SAUCE:
Scant ¼ cup (50 ml) wine vinegar
1 teaspoon Dijon mustard
$5/8$ cup (150 ml) sunflower oil
1 onion, cut in half
½ bunch of flat-leaf parsley
½ bunch of chives
½ bunch of chervil
1 tablespoon capers, crushed
Salt and pepper

Ask your butcher to bone the calf's head (leaving the tongue inside) and to roll and tie it.

The day before, blanch the calf's head: put it in a cooking pot, cover with cold water, and bring to a boil, skimming off impurities regularly. Remove the calf's head from the pot and rinse it.

Peel the carrot and onion. Place the blanched calf's head into a clean cooking pot with the carrot, onion, clove, and bouquet garni and cover with cold water. Salt generously. Bring to a boil, skim off the impurities, then simmer gently for 4 hours. Season to taste with salt.

Once the calf's head is cooked, drain it, reserving some of the cooking broth, and leave to cool. Remove the string, roll it up in plastic wrap and refrigerate overnight.

The next day, prepare the potatoes. Place them in a large pot of cold, salted water and add the peeled garlic clove. Bring to a boil then simmer for about 15 minutes. Check the potatoes are done with the tip of a knife. Drain and peel them while they are still hot.

Make the ravigote. In a bowl, mix the vinegar, mustard, and oil. Finely chop the onion, parsley, chives, chervil and capers, and add to the bowl. Season with salt and pepper.

In a large pot, reheat the cooking broth. Cut the calf's head into quarters, add to the pot with the potatoes, and warm through. Using a slotted spoon, transfer the meat and potatoes to individual dishes, pour over the ravigote sauce, and serve immediately.

Enjoy with an organic Muscadet "Granite" 2017 by Jérôme Bretaudeau.

Travel

WHITE ASPARAGUS
WITH MOUSSELINE SAUCE

SERVES 6

■

PREP: 20 MINUTES
COOK: 20 MINUTES

■

Ingredients

5 ½ lb. (2.5 kg) white
asparagus
Fleur de sel
Freshly ground pepper

FOR THE MOUSSELINE SAUCE:
8 ¾ oz. (250 g) butter
5 egg yolks
3 tablespoons lemon juice
5 tablespoons water
Pinch of Espelette pepper
1 cup (250 ml) very cold whipping cream
Salt

Choose freshly picked asparagus (the stalks should still be moist and if you roll three asparagus spears in your hands, they should squeak.) Peel them carefully by holding them flat by the tip and peeling them in the same direction until you have removed all the skin. Tie the spears in a bunch and steam them for 12 minutes. Check they are done with the tip of a knife (there should be no resistance.)

Make the mousseline sauce. In a small saucepan, melt the butter over very low heat without stirring. Skim off the foam that forms on the surface, retrieve the clarified butter underneath, and leave the whey in the bottom of the pan. In a heatproof bowl placed in a bain-marie over a low heat, emulsify the egg yolks with the lemon juice and water. When the mixture is a little warmer than your finger, remove from the heat and gradually stir in all but 1 tablespoon of the clarified butter, whisking continuously. Season to taste with Espelette pepper and salt. In another bowl, whip the cream. Set aside in the fridge.

Drain the asparagus, lay the spears gently on a clean kitchen towel, and remove the string. Arrange them on the plates and, using a pastry brush, glaze them with the reserved clarified butter. Sprinkle with some fleur de sel crystals and grind over some pepper. Serve the mousseline sauce in a gravy boat with a quenelle of whipped cream on top.

Enjoy with a Pouilly Fumé "Cuvée PurSang" 2015 by Didier Dagueneau.

■

PARMESAN SABLÉ
WITH TOMATO CONFIT AND GOAT CHEESE MOUSSELINE

Ingredients

SERVES 6

■

PREP: 20 MINUTES
REST: 1 HOUR
COOK:
1 HOUR 30 MINUTES

■

FOR THE TOMATO CONFIT:
3 tomatoes
Pinch of superfine sugar
2 teaspoons thyme flowers
1 tablespoon olive oil
Salt and pepper

FOR THE SABLÉS:
$1/3$ cup (2 ¾ oz./80 g)
softened butter, whipped
Scant ½ cup (2 ¾ oz./
80 g) grated Parmesan

$2/3$ cup (2 ¾ oz./80 g)
all-purpose (plain) flour
1 egg yolk, beaten
with 1 teaspoon water

**FOR THE GOAT CHEESE
MOUSSELINE:**
1 ¾ cups (7 oz./200 g)
fresh goat cheese
1 ¼ cups (300 ml)
whipping cream
A few basil leaves, chopped

FOR THE PISTOU:
1 garlic clove
2 bunches of basil
½ tablespoon grated
Parmesan
½ tablespoon pine nuts
Scant ½ cup (100 ml)
olive oil

Make the tomato confit. Preheat the oven to 250°F (120°C). Remove the stalk from the tomatoes and cut a small cross in the skin. Plunge the tomatoes into a pan of simmering water for a few seconds, then immerse them immediately in a bowl of cold water. Remove the skin with a small knife. Cut the tomatoes in half and remove the seeds. Place them face down on a baking sheet, sprinkle with the sugar and thyme flowers, then drizzle with the olive oil. Season with salt and pepper. Cook them in the oven for 3 hours.

Make the sablés. Preheat the oven to 325°F (165°C). In a large bowl, mix the whipped butter, grated Parmesan and flour. Roll out the pastry between two sheets of parchment (greaseproof) paper and cut out six cookies (biscuits). For this, use six separate cookie (pastry) cutters and leave them in place around the sablés until baked. Place the sablés in the refrigerator for 1 hour, then brush them with the beaten egg yolk, using a pastry brush, and bake for 30 minutes. Remove the cookie cutters when the sablés have cooled.

Make the goat cheese mousseline: Put the goat cheese and a scant ¼ cup (50 ml) of the cream in the bowl of a food processor and process until smooth. Whip the remaining cream. Gently mix together the creamy goat cheese and the whipped cream, then stir in the chopped basil. Season with salt and pepper. Set aside in the fridge.

Make the pistou. In a food processor, mix together the garlic, basil, Parmesan and pine nuts, then gradually add the olive oil. If you make the pistou two or three days in advance, the flavors will be even more intense.

To serve, put a little goat cheese mousseline on cold plates and place the sablés on top. Cover with the tomato confit and arrange a large quenelle of the mousseline on top. For a perfectly shaped quenelle, use a hot tablespoon. Drizzle with olive oil. Add a few dots of pistou around the edge of the plate to garnish.

Enjoy with a rosé Bandol "Domaine Tempier" 2018 by the Peyraud family.

STUFFED DOMBES QUAIL
WITH FOIE GRAS AND PORCINI MUSHROOMS

SERVES 6

PREP: 45 MINUTES
COOKING: 1 HOUR

Ingredients

6 Dombes quail, prepared by
your butcher
7 oz. (200 g) porcini mushrooms
(2 ⅔ cups chopped)
2 tablespoons olive oil
¼ cup (1 ¾ oz./50 g) butter +
2 teaspoons for greasing
10 ½ oz. (300 g) sausage stuffing
(see recipe on page 58)
7 oz. (200 g) raw foie gras
7 oz. (200 g) caul fat
2 cups (10 ½ oz./300 g) seedless white grapes
Salt and pepper

FOR THE BANYULS GRAVY:
Reserved quail carcasses, necks, and wings
Scant ¼ cup (50 ml) olive oil
4 teaspoons (¾ oz./20 g) butter
1 shallot
1 onion
1 garlic clove
1 thyme sprig
⅓ cup (80 ml) chicken bouillon
2 tablespoons Banyuls vinegar

FOR THE MASHED POTATO:
(see recipe on page 94)

Ask your butcher to spatchcock the quails and to keep the carcasses, necks, and wings.

Wash and dry the mushrooms, then roughly chop the stems (reserve the caps). Cook the chopped mushroom stems for a few minutes in 1 tablespoon of the olive oil and 4 teaspoons (¾ oz./20 g) of the butter. Leave to cool. In a large bowl, mix the sausage stuffing with the cooled mushrooms. Cut the foie gras into sticks ¾-inch (2-cm) wide and the length of the quail. Season with salt and pepper. Wrap the foie-gras sticks in the stuffing mixture.

Place the quail flat on the work surface, skin side down. Season with salt and pepper and place a stuffing stick along the center of each bird. Close the quails up, returning them to their original shape, and wrap them in caul fat. Set aside in the fridge.

Make the gravy. In a saucepan, sauté the quail carcasses, necks, and wings in the olive oil for a few minutes. Add the butter and mix to loosen the cooking residues from the bottom of the pan. Chop the shallot and onion and score the garlic cloves by making several small cuts along the sides. Add to the pan, along with the thyme. Let it cook, stirring constantly. Drain everything in a colander, reserving the cooking fat. Wipe out the pan, put everything (except the cooking fat) back into it and pour in the chicken bouillon. Heat and leave to reduce for about 15 minutes, until the gravy has thickened. Season with salt and pepper. Strain through a fine mesh sieve and add the vinegar. Keep warm.

Preheat the oven to 280°F (140°C) and butter a roasting pan. Place the quail in the pan and season with salt and pepper. Brush the quail with the reserved cooking fat and roast in the oven for 20 minutes. Cover the quail with foil and let them rest in the oven with the door open.

Cut the mushroom caps into large pieces. Season with salt and pepper. Fry the mushrooms in 1 tablespoon of olive oil and 2 tablespoons (30 g) of butter. Keep warm. Peel the grapes and panfry them in 1 teaspoon of olive oil. Keep warm.

To serve, place some mashed potato on the warm plates, cut each quail at an angle so that the stuffing is clearly visible and lay it on top. Arrange some porcini mushrooms and grapes, and then pour over some gravy.

Enjoy with a Vosne-Romanée Village "Domaine d'Eugénie" 2009 by Artémis Domaines.

CRISPY WHITING "PAPILLOTES"
WITH AVOCADO

SERVES 6

·

PREP: 45 MINUTES
COOK: 25 MINUTES

·

Ingredients

3 line-caught whiting
(each about 2 lb./900 g)
2 very ripe avocados
1 lime
¼ red onion, finely chopped
Pinch of Espelette pepper
1 bunch of coriander, leaves chopped
½ cup (100ml) olive oil

3 round sheets of filo dough
Scant ¼ cup (1 ¾ oz./50 g)
melted butter
5 oz. (150 g) piquillo peppers
4 ¼ cups (1 l) sunflower oil
Fleur de sel and salt

Ask your fishmonger to fillet the whiting and remove any small bones, then to cut the fillets into fairly thick strips.

Peel the avocados, put the flesh into a small bowl, add the lime juice, and crush with a fork. Stir in the onion, Espelette pepper, coriander, and half of the olive oil. Season to taste with salt. Set aside in the fridge.

Lay the dough sheets flat on the work surface and cut out six small triangles. Using a pastry brush, spread a thin layer of melted butter on each triangle, then place half a piquillo pepper and a piece of whiting in the center of each. Roll up into a crescent shape. Make all the "papillotes" in the same way then refrigerate them.

Divide the avocado among the plates. Set aside in the fridge.

Pour the sunflower oil into a deep-fat fryer and heat to 335°F (170°C). Immerse each papillote in the oil and fry for 2–3 minutes. Drain the papillotes on paper towels then place them, hot, onto the chilled avocado puree. Drizzle over some olive oil, sprinkle with a little fleur de sel, and serve immediately.

Enjoy with a gin and tonic made with Monkey 47 gin, Fever-Tree tonic water, and some crushed juniper berries.

FINE SOLE MEUNIÈRE

SERVES 6

▪

PREP: 15 MINUTES
COOK: 4 HOURS 20 MINUTES

▪

Ingredients

3 sole (each about 1 lb. 2 oz./500 g),
prepared by your fishmonger
½ cup (2 ¼ oz./60 g) all-purpose flour
Scant ½ cup (100 ml) olive oil
Generous ¾ cup (6 ½ oz./185 g)
slightly salted butter
3 lemons

FOR THE MASHED POTATO
(see recipe on page 94)

Ask your fishmonger to prepare the sole (i.e. gut them, remove the black skin, and scrape the white skin to remove the scales). Rinse the sole in cold water and dry them carefully with paper towels. Flour both sides and pat them over a plate to remove any excess.

Heat the olive oil in a skillet, and gently lay a sole, skin side down, in the pan. When it is beginning to color, add the butter and lower the heat: the butter should foam but not blacken. Turn the sole over and keep spooning over the butter. Stick a piece of raw spaghetti into the fish to check it is cooked: it should pierce the flesh through the bones. Once all the sole are cooked, turn the heat up and let the butter color lightly. When it begins to release a hazelnutty aroma, turn off the heat and add the lemon juice.

Fillet the sole, place two fillets on each plate, and top with the butter sauce. Serve with the mashed potato and a lemon half.

Enjoy with a Bouzy Rouge 2017 by Georges Vesselle.

THE SUPPLIERS

Although it's the skill of La Fontaine de Mars's chef that has made the place famous, the high value it places in fine produce also has a lot to do with its success. Christiane and Jacques Boudon, like the chef, insist on only the very best produce, and they rely on their eyes and their instincts to tell them when they've found it. And when a surprise discovery leads to trust in a supplier becoming established, they're unwaveringly loyal to them.

PHILIPPE NOYÉ, JEAN-LUC LAVATINE, AND SEBASTIEN PRADAL, WINE AGENTS, AND PIERRE BÉROT

Christiane calls them her "fiancés" (boyfriends), and she has enjoyed an idyllic relationship with these "three musketeers" of fine wine for years. Their range is vast and often full of surprises. And even after all this time, they can often still amaze each other. On the one hand, they bring Christiane unconventional wines that surprise her; on the other, she sometimes shows more boldness in her tastes than they expect from her.

Christiane Boudon was very young when she first met Philippe Noyé, known to everyone in the world of winemakers and restaurateurs by the nickname "Ma Poule." From the Lozère, he is an agent for winemakers whose wines grace the tables of many Michelin-starred restaurants. Having worked as a sommelier at Pierre Gagnaire's restaurant in Saint-Etienne, then in Paris, Jean-Luc Lavatine switched sides and began selling fine Bordeaux wines; it is thanks to his precious advice that Christiane Boudon has acquired her greatest grands crus classés. As for Sebastien Pradal, who is from Aveyron, he introduced Christiane to his southwestern roots by giving her a taste for wines with which she was quite unfamiliar. And she's very happy to have made their acquaintance. Lastly, there is Pierre Bérot, who is from Bagnères-de-Bigorre, in the Pyrenees. He was a sommelier and a buyer with the Taillevent group before becoming General Manager of Duclot, the sanctuary for the great wines of Bordeaux. As such, he has been responsible for many of Christiane's early discoveries in wine and winemaking. Assisted by these four advocates of fine wine, Christiane Boudon has refined her palate and structured her tastes over the years. If, today, she can boast of having the flair to compose the restaurant's cellar, it's undoubtedly thanks to these brilliant talent scouts.

LE COQ SAINT-HONORÉ AND LES BOUCHERIES NIVERNAISES

Meat and poultry have a prominent place on the menu at
La Fontaine de Mars. The chef finds his celebrated poultry
at Le Coq Saint-Honoré, while his supplies of beef, pork,
and veal come from Les Boucheries Nivernaises. These two
renowned establishments are both run by the Bissonnet
family since it acquired Le Coq Saint-Honoré a short while
ago. Working hand-in-hand with the greatest restaurateurs,
this family of connoisseurs has treated meat lovers to
the very finest produce for three generations. At Coq
Saint-Honoré, the poultry comes from Bresse or Gâtinais
and has impeccable credentials. Likewise, the fine pedigree
of the veal, pork and beef of Les Boucheries Nivernaises
guarantees premium meat. All of this means that
La Fontaine de Mars is able to ensure the consistent high
quality of its signature dishes. Meanwhile, there's nothing
like an exceptional arrival of a whole pork loin to enthuse
the chef and get his imagination working on creating
a new dish for the day's specials.

**THERE'S NOTHING LIKE
AN EXCEPTIONAL ARRIVAL
OF A WHOLE PORK LOIN
TO ENTHUSE THE CHEF
AND GET HIS IMAGINATION
WORKING ON CREATING
A NEW DISH FOR THE DAY'S
SPECIALS.**

THIERRY LEMÉTAYER, FISHERMAN'S AGENT

Métayer is the "Monsieur Poisson" of La Fontaine de Mars, the person who forms the link between the restaurant and the Breton fishermen. Several times a week, he selects the finest freshly caught fish and shellfish before heading to the capital to drop off his precious haul at the restaurant's kitchens in the early morning. It's common for him and the chef to talk to each other late at night to take stock of what has just entered the port: a catch from small boats with a mixture of scorpion fish, pollock, and small fish; rope-grown mussels; open-sea oysters from Morlaix bay, which are particularly salty because they're not mellowed in fresh water. And then there are magnificent lobsters, which arrive at the restaurant still alive, and scallops, quivering with freshness. While Thierry Métayer makes an inventory of what he has in his nets, the chef is letting loose his imagination and mentally creating the next day's menu. It's a happy improvisation, inspired by this astute envoy, who, very aware of what's required, offers the chef only the very best.

WHILE THIERRY LEMÉTAYER MAKES AN INVENTORY OF WHAT HE HAS IN HIS NETS, THE CHEF IS LETTING LOOSE HIS IMAGINATION AND MENTALLY CREATING THE NEXT DAY'S MENU. IT'S A HAPPY IMPROVISATION, INSPIRED BY THIS ASTUTE ENVOY, WHO, VERY AWARE OF WHAT'S REQUIRED, OFFERS THE CHEF ONLY THE VERY BEST.

HAVING WORKED FOR LA FONTAINE DE MARS FOR YEARS, GÉRARD AND JULIEN IOLI KNOW BY HEART CHRISTIANE BOUDON AND CHEF PIERRE SAUGRAIN'S DESIRE AND REQUIREMENTS FOR EXCEPTIONAL PRODUCE.

GÉRARD AND JULIEN IOLI, MARKET GARDENERS

Market gardening has become a family affair in the Ioli family, since Julien, the son, has taken an active role in his father Gérard's business. For La Fontaine de Mars, they are also a source of sumptuous regional produce, because the Iolis are no ordinary local market gardeners. Located in the 7th arrondissement of Paris, not far from the restaurant, they have developed a retail-wholesale business and undertake to unearth fruits and vegetables in the region surrounding Paris and throughout France that will help their customers create wonderful dishes.

Having worked for La Fontaine de Mars for years, Gérard and Julien Ioli know by heart Christiane Boudon and chef Pierre Saugrain's desire and requirements for exceptional produce. In fact, it's not uncommon to find the restaurant's owner or chef in the Ioli's cold room, fascinated by the very fresh bunches of colorful radishes or asparagus, bent over the crates like gold-diggers getting their hands on treasure. Some days, it will be the wild strawberries or raspberries that get them excited. On others, the magnificent morel mushrooms that fire their enthusiasm. At La Fontaine de Mars, the journey of the senses begins in this Aladdin's cave.

STUFFED PORK LOIN
WITH PORCINI MUSHROOMS, SERVED WITH TRUFFLE JUS

SERVES 6
·

PREP: 1 HOUR
COOK: 2 HOURS 40 MINUTES
·

Ingredients

6 double pork loin chops (each about
12 ¼ oz./350 g)
7 oz. (200 g) caul fat

FOR THE TRUFFLE JUS:
1 shallot
2 garlic cloves
10 ½ oz. (300 g) blade shoulder of pork,
cut into pieces
Scant ¼ cup (50 ml) olive oil
A few thyme sprigs
3 ½ tablespoons (1 ¾ oz./50 g) butter
1 teaspoon bitter cocoa powder
2 cups (500 ml) chicken bouillon
1 ½ oz. (40 g) black truffle shavings
Dash of sherry vinegar

FOR THE STUFFING:
1 lb. 2 oz. (500 g) porcini mushrooms
2 ¼ oz. (60 g) cured ham, finely diced
1 shallot, finely diced
½ tablespoon olive oil
2 tablespoons (30 g) butter
$^5/_8$ cup (150 ml) whipping cream
2 teaspoons Dijon mustard
½ bunch of chives, chopped
Salt and pepper

FOR THE HERB SALAD:
1 ¾ oz. (50 g) corn salad
1 ¾ oz. (50 g) curly endive
(with a yellow heart)
½ bunch of chervil
½ bunch of tarragon
½ bunch of dill
½ bunch of flat-leaf parsley
A few lemon balm leaves
½ bunch of chives,
cut into 2-inch (5-cm) lengths

■

Make the jus. Finely dice the shallot. Score the unpeeled garlic cloves by making several small cuts along the sides so the flavor diffuses. In a casserole, fry the pork shoulder in olive oil, then add the shallots, garlic, and thyme. Add the butter to loosen the cooking residues from the bottom of the pan without burning. Strain the contents of the casserole through a fine mesh sieve and set aside this cooking butter. Wipe the casserole to remove all the fat, then put the sieve contents back into it. Fry on a high heat and add the bitter cocoa to dry the fat. Pour in a little chicken bouillon to deglaze, then add the remainder. Cover and simmer for 1 hour 30 minutes.

Make the stuffing. Peel, clean, and dry the porcini mushrooms. Separate the caps from the stems and dice. In another casserole, brown the diced ham and shallot in the olive oil and butter. Add the mushrooms and reduce until all the cooking juices have evaporated. Add the cream and reduce until the sauce is fairly thick. Turn off the heat, then stir in the mustard and chopped chives. Season with salt and pepper. Set aside in the fridge.

Preheat the oven to 300°F (150°C). Using a knife, make a small incision in the pork loin chops, opposite the bone, to create a cavity inside the meat. Carefully fill the chops with the stuffing up to the bone, then wrap in caul fat (closing it opposite the incision). Roast the pork in the oven for 20–25 minutes, turning carefully and basting with the reserved cooking butter. Remove the meat from the oven and let it rest.

Prepare the herb salad. With your hands, gently toss together the corn salad, curly endive, chervil, tarragon, dill, flat-leaf parsley, lemon balm, and chives. Set aside in the fridge.

Reduce the jus in a saucepan then strain it through a fine mesh sieve. Season with salt and pepper. Add the chopped truffle and sherry vinegar to add a note of acidity. Keep the jus warm.

To serve, arrange the herb salad on the plates. Cut the pork loin chops into two so that the stuffing it clearly visible and lay them on top of the salad. Pour over the truffle jus, which will also season the herb salad.

Enjoy with a Vacqueyras Le Sang des Cailloux "Cuvée Lopy" 2013 by the Férigoule Family.

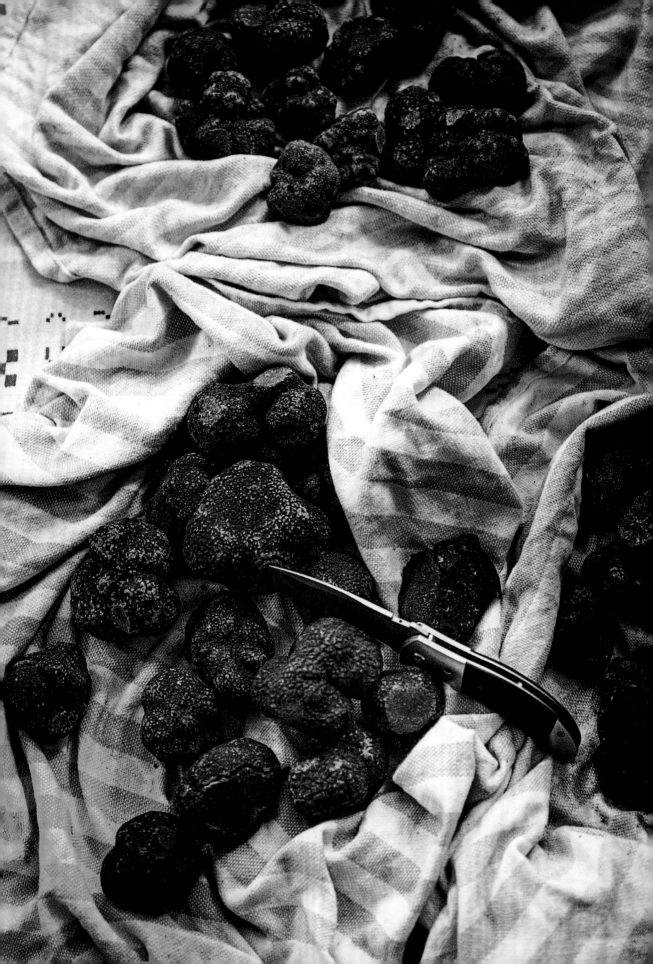

SCALLOPS
WITH WELL-SEASONED CHICKEN JUS, JERUSALEM ARTICHOKE MOUSSELINE, AND BLACK TRUFFLES

SERVES 6

·

PREP: 30 MINUTES
REST: 12 HOURS
COOK: 3 HOURS

·

Ingredients

FOR THE SCALLOPS:
13 lb. (6 kg) Normandy scallops in their shells
1/6 oz. (5 g) black truffle
Scant ½ cup (100 ml) olive oil
¼ cup (2 ¼ oz./60 g) butter

FOR THE CHICKEN JUS:
2 ¼ lb. (1 kg) chicken wings, cut into small pieces by your butcher
Scant ½ cup (100 ml) olive oil
2 ¾ tablespoons (1 ½ oz./40 g) butter
½ onion
½ shallot
1 garlic clove
3 thyme sprigs
4 ¼ cups (1 l) chicken bouillon

FOR THE JERUSALEM ARTICHOKE MOUSSELINE
3 ¼ lb. (1.5 kg) of Jerusalem artichokes
2 tablespoons (30 g) butter
1 scant cup (200 ml) whipping cream
Scant ¼ cup (50 ml) olive oil
Salt and pepper

The day before, ask your fishmonger to prepare the scallops and remove the coral. Wash them under cold running water, dry them carefully, then slice them widthwise without separating the two halves. Cut the truffle into thin strips with a truffle mandolin and slide a strip into each scallop. Refrigerate overnight.

The next day, make the chicken jus. In a casserole, brown the chicken wings in the olive oil for a few minutes. Add the butter, let it foam, and loosen the cooking residues from the bottom of the pan with a wooden spoon. Chop the onion and shallot and score the garlic cloves by making several small cuts along the sides. Add to the pan, along with the thyme. Let it cook, stirring constantly. Strain through a fine mesh sieve, wipe out the pan, then return everything to the pan and pour in the chicken bouillon.

Reduce over low heat for about 2 hours, until the jus has thickened. Season with salt and pepper. Strain the jus through a fine mesh sieve and keep warm.

Make the Jerusalem artichoke mousseline. Peel the Jerusalem artichokes and steam them for 30 minutes. Drain, then puree them, adding the butter and the cream to obtain a smooth but not too runny puree. Season with salt and pepper. Keep warm.

Sear the scallops on both sides in a hot skillet with the olive oil, then lower the heat and add the butter. Drain the scallops on paper towels and keep them warm.

To serve, place two big spoons of Jerusalem artichoke mousseline in the center of the hot plates, arrange the scallops on top, and pour over the chicken jus.

Enjoy with a Pouilly Fuissé "Clos Reyssié" 2015 by Dominique Cornin.

BORN UNDER A LUCKY STAR

The restaurant business is Pierre Saugrain's life. The son of established restaurant owners in Vernon, Eure (in northern France), he got caught up in their enthusiasm and, from the age of eleven, would cook up fine dishes for his parents on Sundays. A few years later, his father sent him off to Les Quatre Saisons, the Michelin-starred restaurant of the Hôtel de Dieppe in Rouen, to learn the ropes. There, he obtained his certificate of professional competence before crossing the Channel to learn English techniques at the Four Seasons in London for a year. Back in France, the Sofitel des Invalides, in Paris, gave him the opportunity to work in the Dauphin's kitchens alongside chef Jacques Hébert, a former sous-chef to Joël Robuchon. Thereafter, he followed a star-studded career path, including at Au Trou Gascon, Carré des Feuillants, and Le Miraville, famous for its southwestern cuisine. These experiences provided him with what turned out to be a rigorous and excellent education, where even the hectic pace of his working days could not tarnish the happiness he felt in working alongside some great and inspiring chefs.

ICONIC SIGNATURE DISHES

You need only cast your eye over the tables at La Fontaine de Mars to understand that the star of the show is its cassoulet. This famous dish, before being "French," is first and foremost an iconic specialty of the gastronomy of the South West, and people come from all over the world to savor it here. Because La Fontaine de Mars is to cassoulet what Joël Robuchon is to mashed potatoes: the benchmark. Saugrain's secret? A perfect alchemy between magnificent homemade sausage and duck confit, sublime Tarbais beans (a southwestern cannellini-like bean) and exquisite garlic sausage, all intensified with a pinch of Espelette pepper, which the chef and his team know how to measure out perfectly.

This legendary southwestern dish sits on La Fontaine de Mars' menu alongside other signature dishes. The chicken with morel mushrooms is an essential dish that English and American guests are particularly fond of. Passionate about using only the best ingredients, the chef gives his chicken with morel mushrooms extraordinary flavors, including a dash of Monbazillac that asserts the character of the poultry. When morels are in season, he prepares preserves in brine that will delight devotees of the dish throughout the year.

TENDER PIG CHEEKS
WITH FOIE GRAS, ORANGE JUS, AND ARTICHOKE

SERVES 6

PREP: 45 MINUTES
COOK: 3 HOUR 30 MINUTES

Ingredients

12 free-range pig cheeks
1 tablespoon olive oil
1 scant cup (200 ml) concentrated orange juice
Scant ½ cup packed (3 ½ oz./ 100 g) brown sugar
1 orange, cut into quarters

$5/8$ cup (150 ml) sherry vinegar
$5/8$ cup (150 ml) veal bouillon
6 artichokes
4 teaspoons (¾ oz./20 g) butter
6 raw duck foie gras cutlets (each about 1 ½ oz./40 g)
Scant ½ cup (100 ml) olive oil
Salt and pepper

Salt and pepper the pork cheeks, then brown them in a pan with the olive oil. Set aside.

Pour the orange juice and and brown sugar into a saucepan, add the orange quarters, and heat until the sugar begins to caramelize. When the mixture begins to color, stop the cooking by pouring in a scant ½ cup (100 ml) of sherry vinegar. Bring to a boil again, pour in the veal juice, and simmer to reduce. Season with salt and pepper.

Preheat the oven to 225°F (110°C). Place the pork cheeks in a baking dish, pour over the orange jus with the orange quarters, then cook in the oven for 2 hours.

Steam the artichokes for 50 minutes. Leave to cool, then remove the leaves and choke to leave only the artichoke bottoms. Cut them into pieces and panfry them in the butter.

Remove the pork cheeks from the oven and drain them and reduce the sauce in a pan until syrupy. Stir in the remaining sherry vinegar.

In an attractive casserole dish, layer the pork cheeks and panfried artichokes, cover with the sauce and warm in the oven at 325°F (165°C) for 15 minutes.

Meanwhile, panfry the foie gras cutlets in a nonstick skillet without adding fat. Remove the casserole from the oven and lay the foie gras cutlets on top before serving at the table.

Enjoy with a dry white Pacherenc "Château Montus" 2012 by Alain Brumont.

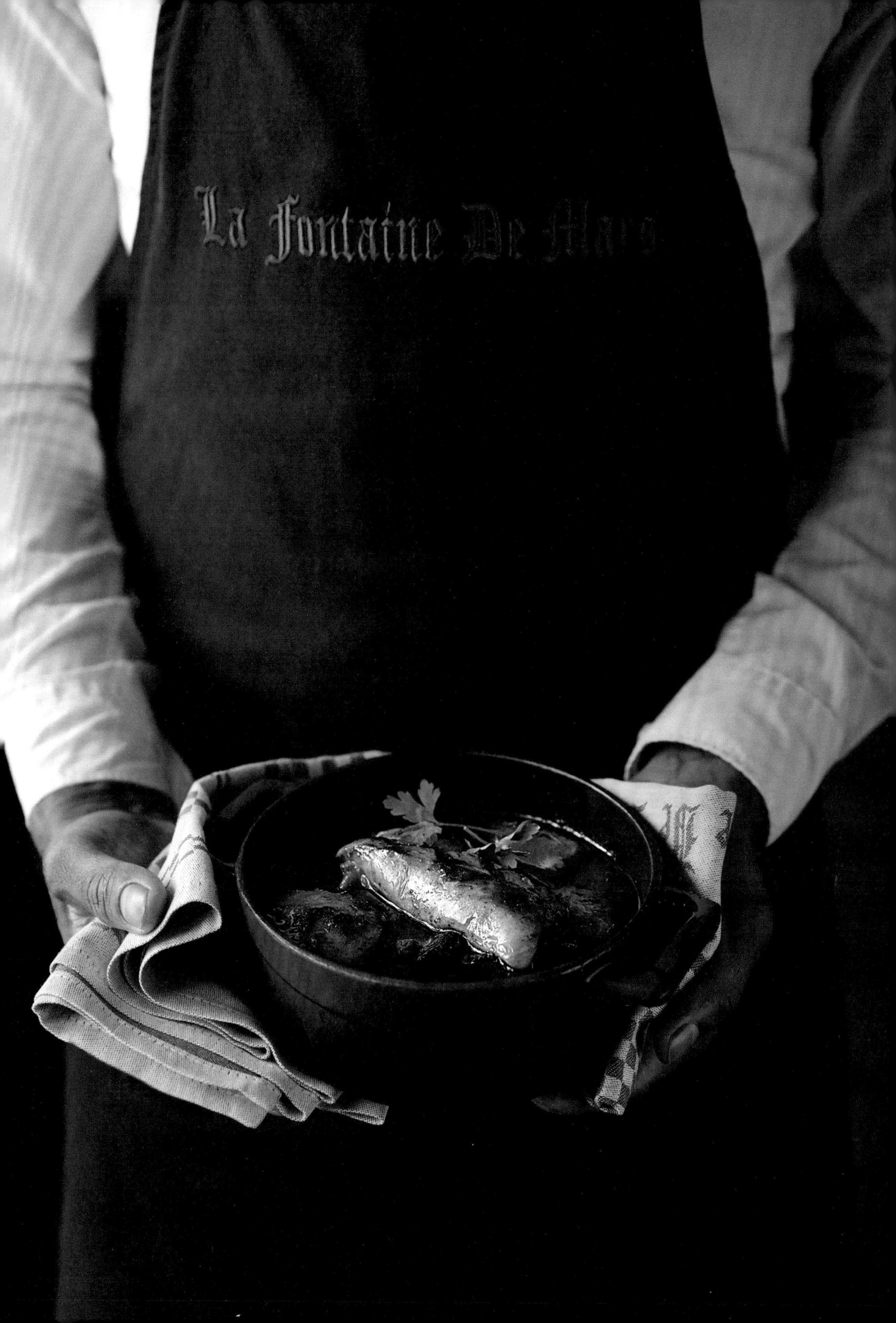
La Fontaine De

There is also the famous lièvre à la royale, an exceptional dish that few restaurants venture to put on their menu. Pierre Saugrain was not one to retreat from the challenge, however, even though the rich associations and distinctive flavors of hare seem to go against current trends. The hare is cooked with foie gras, truffles, porcini mushrooms, and sweetbreads and enhanced with a touch of Armagnac. The ingredients may be off-putting to some customers, but the serving staff are the chef's ambassadors and have learned how to explain this complex dish to curious diners. And so, hare à la royale has become part of the restaurant's DNA. Today, its devotees would sell their souls to enjoy this princely dish, which has been restored to its former prestige largely thanks to Pierre Saugrain. Indeed, when great aficionados of lièvre à la royale compare his version to those of triple-Michelin-starred restaurants, the chef prides himself on having followed his intuition.

In fact, the chef loves nothing more than setting himself challenges. For some time, the desire to do something to improve the often-maligned image of pork loin had been gnawing away at him. Too dry, say its critics. Not if you put your skill and your heart into cooking it, maintains Saugrain. And he has proved it. The very thickly cut loin is opened up on one side and stuffed with a generous, rich filling of porcini mushrooms cooked in cream. While the meat is roasting in the oven, the cream tenderizes the meat, which far from becoming dry, is slowly infused with delicate mushroom aromas. The judicious but simple salad of aromatic herbs enhanced with a truffle-flavored jus that accompanies it does the rest. He has won the bet: those who formerly maligned pork loin find themselves eating their words once they've tasted Sauguin's unique version! Pork loin stuffed with porcini mushrooms has now joined the ranks of the restaurant's signature recipes.

As have the porcini mushroom pâté, the boudin, the duck confit, and the legendary brawn, all of which sell themselves, according to the chef. He adds that when the kitchen runs out of the pork loin, customers will express their disappointment with him. After all, they consider themselves at home here.

The same is true with the desserts: Saugrain has enhanced the great classics with his baba flavored with sweet, strong rum, his vanilla mille-feuille, his chocolate mousse served with a crunchy coffee cone, his divinely light floating island, and his vanilla crème brûlée. With his virtuoso touch and that of his teams, these iconic French desserts are transformed into masterpieces of panache, elegance and gourmet pleasure.

BRAISED BEEF CHEEKS
WITH MADIRAN WINE SAUCE AND TENDER CARROTS

SERVES 6

∎

PREP: 45 MINUTES
COOK:
4 HOURS 30 MINUTES

∎

Ingredients

FOR THE WINE SAUCE:
4 ¼ cups (1 l) Madiran red wine
1 bouquet garni
8 cups (2 l) veal bouillon
Pinch of superfine sugar
1 teaspoon wine vinegar
Salt and pepper

FOR THE BEEF CHEEKS:
2 untrimmed beef cheeks
¼ cup (2 ¼ oz./60 g) butter
1 scant cup (200 ml) olive oil
1 carrot
1 onion
1 shallot
Peel of 1 orange
1 bouquet garni
Scant ½ cup (100 ml) chicken bouillon

FOR THE CARROTS:
6 large sand-grown carrots
Scant ½ cup (100 ml) chicken bouillon
Pinch of sugar
¼ cup (2 ¼ oz./60 g) butter

Make the wine sauce. In a small sauce-pan, reduce the red wine with the bouquet garni until you are left with just a thin film of wine in the bottom of the pan. Add the veal bouillon and let simmer. Stop cooking when the mixture coats the spoon. Season with salt and pepper. Stir in the sugar and vinegar, then strain the sauce through a fine mesh sieve. Keep warm.

Prepare the beef cheeks. Season the meat. Heat the butter and half the olive oil in a skillet, then brown the cheeks on all sides. They should be well colored with a crust. Set aside.

Peel and dice the carrot, onion, and shallot. Sauté them in a casserole with the remaining olive oil, then add the orange peel and bouquet garni. Add the beef cheeks and pour in the wine sauce. Let reduce, pour in the chicken broth, and bring back to a boil.

Preheat the oven to 250°F (120°C). Cover the casserole and place in the oven for 3–4 hours. The meat should be very tender and beginning to fall apart.

Meanwhile, prepare the carrots. Peel them and cut them into pieces. Put them in a saucepan and pour in the chicken bouillon. Add the sugar and butter, season with salt and pepper, then cook for about 40 minutes, until the bouillon has almost completely evaporated. The carrots will be very tender and glossy.

Serve the beef cheeks and tender carrots in soup plates. Adjust the seasoning of the cooking sauce, strain it through a fine mesh sieve, and pour it over the beef cheeks and carrots. Grind over some pepper and serve immediately.

Enjoy with a Cahors "Cuvée Dame Honneur du Château Lagrézette" 2012 by Alain-Dominique Perrin.

SUNDAY ROAST CHICKEN

SERVES 6

·

PREP: 15 MINUTES
REST: 24 HOURS
COOK: 1 HOUR 10 MINUTES

·

Ingredients

FOR THE ROAST CHICKEN:
1 garlic clove
2 ¼ oz. (60 g) softened butter
¼ onion
½ shallot
1 thyme sprig
1 bay leaf
1 free-range chicken of about
4 ½ lb. (2 kg), gutted
2 tablespoons olive oil
Salt and pepper

FOR THE GRAVY:
1 tablespoon white wine
Scant ½ cup (100 ml)
chicken bouillon
1 tablespoon water
1 tablespoon vinegar mustard
1 ½ tablespoons (1 oz./25 g) butter

FOR THE MASHED POTATO
(see recipe on page 94)

The day before, prepare the chicken. Score the garlic cloves by making several small cuts along the sides and place in a bowl. Add the softened butter, onion, shallot, thyme leaves, and bay leaf and mix together well. Stuff the chicken with this mixture and refrigerate for 24 hours.

The next day, preheat the oven to 360°F (180°C). Massage the chicken flesh with the olive oil. Season with salt and pepper. Roast the chicken in the oven, basting it every 5 minutes for the duration of cooking: 20 minutes on one leg, 20 minutes on the other leg, and 20 minutes turned on its back after lowering the oven temperature to 325°F (160°C). Remove the chicken from the oven and turn off the oven. Cover the dish with foil and leave to rest in the oven with the door open for 20 minutes.

Make the gravy. Deglaze the roasting pan with the white wine to loosen all the cooking residues from the bottom of the pan, then stir in the bouillon, water, and mustard. Strain this gravy through a fine mesh sieve into a small saucepan and, over low heat, whisk in the butter.

Carve the roast chicken and serve it with the mashed potato. Pour over the gravy and serve immediately.

Enjoy with a Beaujolais-Villages "Le Rang du Merle" 2016 by Jean-Claude Lapalu.

THE TASTE FOR ADVENTURE

While the menu remains unchanging and traditionally rooted in the terroir, the chef gives free rein to his imagination with the specials of the day, which are often more audacious. Saugrain creates instinctively and has a visceral need to improvise and innovate, and he allows the exceptional freshness of the fine produce to guide his imagination. He never moves too far from the basics—that would be playing with fire—but he loves experimenting, and especially with spices and seasonings, knowledge of which his Sri Lankan, West Indian and Japanese sous-chefs have on the tip of their tongue. Used subtly, they allow him to play around with the classics without confusing the taste buds of his regulars.

He has also created some fine desserts, including his sublime, and brightly colored, strawberries with vanilla and pistachio zabaglione. Over the years, this has become a restaurant classic that delights those with a sweet tooth throughout the summer.

Specials of the day are a great success at La Fontaine de Mars and never linger long on the menu board. So, it's best to arrive early to enjoy these momentary inspirations, which are usually available only that day.

RUM BABA
WITH WHIPPED CREAM

SERVES 6

PREP: 20 MINUTES
REST: 50 MINUTES
COOK: 45 MINUTES

Ingredients

FOR THE SYRUP:
4 ¼ cups (1 l) water
2 ½ cups (1 lb. 2 oz./500 g)
superfine sugar
1 orange
1 lemon
1 Bourbon vanilla bean

FOR THE RUM BABA:
½ cup (3 ¾ oz./110 g) butter
+ 1 tablespoon for the mold
2 cups (8 ¾ oz./250 g)
all-purpose flour +
1 tablespoon for
the work surface
4 teaspoons (12 g)
active dry yeast

4 teaspoons (12 ml) milk
2 eggs, beaten
2 tablespoons apricot glaze
Clement aged rum

FOR THE WHIPPED CREAM:
1 ¼ cups (300 ml)
whipping cream
1 Bourbon vanilla bean

Make the syrup. In a saucepan, heat the water and sugar, then add the orange and lemon. Leave the fruits whole but score the peel so that their aromas are diffused in the syrup. Add the split and scraped vanilla bean, reserving the seeds. Bring to a boil on a high heat, stir, then immediately remove from the heat.

Make the rum baba. Preheat the oven to 325°F (165°C). In a saucepan, melt the butter and let it cool. Sift the flour and yeast into a bowl. In another saucepan, slightly warm the milk, then pour it over the flour and yeast mixture. Add the eggs and the cold melted butter. Mix to form a ball and roll this dough on a floured surface with the palm of your hand. Place the dough in a buttered savarin mold and leave it near a heat source until it has risen nearly to the top of the mold. Bake it in the oven for 25 minutes, being careful that the top doesn't burn. Unmold the baba and leave it to cool.

Heat, but don't boil, the syrup and soak the baba in it for about 30 minutes, turning it and spooning the syrup over it regularly. Drain the baba on a wire rack.

In a saucepan, heat the apricot glaze with a little water to dilute it, then pour a very thin coating over the baba.

Make the whipped cream. Whip the cream with the vanilla bean seeds until firm.

Cut the baba into slices and arrange two slices on each plate. Add a tablespoon of syrup and pipe over some vanilla cream. Drizzle with the rum and serve.

Enjoy with a glass of Zacapa 23 Year Old rum from Guatemala.

LEMON MERINGUE PIE

Ingredients

SERVES 6

■

PREP: 30 MINUTES
REST: 30 HOURS
COOK: 25 MINUTES

■

FOR THE SWEET PIE DOUGH:
2 cups (8 ¾ oz./250 g)
all-purpose flour
Pinch of salt
3 egg yolks
½ cup (3 ½ oz./100 g)
superfine sugar
1 tablespoon cold water
Generous ½ cup
(4 ½ oz./125 g) softened
butter

FOR THE LEMON CREAM:
2 sheets of gelatin
¾ cup (175 ml) lemon juice
1 ¼ cups (8 ¾ oz./250 g)
superfine sugar
½ cup + 2 teaspoons
(4 ½ oz./125 g) melted butter
6 eggs

FOR THE MERINGUE:
3 ½ oz. (100 g) egg white
(about 3 whites)
¾ cup unsifted (3 ½ oz./
100 g) confectioners' sugar
1 untreated lime

The day before, make the sweet pie dough. Place the flour, salt, egg yolks, sugar, and cold water in the bowl of a food-processor and pulse until the mixture forms a ball. Add the butter, cut into small pieces. Put the dough in a bowl, cover with a clean kitchen towel, and refrigerate for 24 hours.

The next day, remove the dough from the fridge and leave to stand for 20 minutes before rolling it out to a thickness of ½inch (1 cm). Use the dough to line a pie plate, leaving a thick rim, and refrigerate for 3 hours.

Preheat the oven to 350°C (170°C). Cover the bottom of the pie plate with foil and fill with pie weights. Bake for 15 minutes, then remove the foil and pie weights and bake for a further 5 minutes. Allow the pie shell to cool.

Make the lemon cream. Soften the gelatin sheets in a bowl of cold water for 3 minutes. Strain the lemon juice through a fine mesh sieve into a bowl and add the sugar, melted butter, and eggs. Place in a bain-marie over medium heat and whisk constantly until the mixture is thick and creamy. Remove from heat and add the well-drained gelatin leaves. Stir to mix, then pour the lemon cream into the pie shell. Cover with plastic wrap (and refrigerate for 3 hours).

Make the meringue. Whisk the egg whites with the confectioners' sugar. Carefully spoon this meringue mixture into a piping bag fitted with a large star tip and completely cover the pie with large drops of meringue. Just before serving the lemon meringue pie, caramelize the meringue quickly with a kitchen blowtorch.

Enjoy with a slightly smoked and well-infused black tea from Maison Mariage Frères.

183

VANILLA MILLEFEUILLES

Ingredients

1 lb. 5 oz. (600 g) puff pastry from your baker

FOR CRÈME PÂTISSIÈRE:
2 cups (500 ml) milk
1 Bourbon vanilla bean
5 egg yolks
Scant ½ cup (3 ¼ oz./90 g) superfine sugar
½ cup (2 ½ oz./70 g) all-purpose flour
2 teaspoons confectioners' sugar
1 cup (250 ml) whipping cream

SERVES 6

■

PREP: 20 MINUTES
COOK: 45 MINUTES

■

Preheat the oven to 350°C (170°C). Roll out the puff pastry to a thickness of ½ an inch (1 cm) and place on a baking sheet. Cover with another baking sheet and top with evenly distributed weights to prevent the pastry from rising too much. Bake in the oven for 15 minutes. Set aside.

Make the crème pâtissière. In a saucepan, heat the milk with the split and scraped vanilla bean. In a bowl, whisk the egg yolks with the superfine sugar until they turn white, then sift in the flour and combine. Pour in a ladle of hot milk to thin the mixture, then pour it into the pan. Cook without stirring for 10 minutes. Leave the crème pâtissière to cool, stirring it regularly to prevent a skin forming on top. Set aside in the fridge.

Preheat the oven broiler. Sprinkle the puff pastry with confectioners' sugar, using a sifter to ensure you get a thin, even layer. Place the baking sheet under the broiler, keeping an eye on it to ensure that the sugar doesn't burn. Leave to cool, then sprinkle with another layer of confectioners' sugar and return it to the broiler. Repeat this process a third time so that the pastry is well caramelized.

Whip the cream until firm and fold it into the crème pâtissière. Cut eighteen regular rectangles from the puff pastry and assemble the millefeuilles: completely cover one rectangle with small dots of cream using a piping bag, cover with another pastry rectangle, then repeat the process, finishing with a pastry rectangle. Sprinkle the millefeuilles with confectioners' sugar just before serving.

Enjoy with a well-chilled Ruinart Blanc de Blancs Champagne.

HOMEMADE BRIOCHE FRENCH TOAST
WITH VANILLA MOUSSELINE AND RED BERRIES

SERVES 6

▪

PREPARATION : 15 MINUTES
COOK : 50 MINUTES

▪

Ingredients

FOR FOR THE BRIOCHE:
½ cup (3 ¾ oz./110 g) butter
+ 1 tablespoon for the mold
2 cups (8 ¾ oz./250 g)
all-purpose flour +
1 tablespoon for the work
surface
4 teaspoons (12 g)
active dry yeast
2 teaspoons milk
2 eggs, beaten
2 tablespoons superfine
sugar for the mold +
2 tablespoons for the top
of the brioche

FOR THE FRENCH TOAST:
1 cup (250 ml) whole milk
1 cup (250 ml) whipping cream
½ cup (3 ½ oz./100 g)
superfine sugar
1 whole egg + 2 yolks
2 ¾ tablespoons
(1 ½ oz./40 g) butter
6 pinches of brown sugar

FOR THE VANILLA MOUSSELINE:
1 ¼ cups (300 ml) milk
½ Bourbon vanilla bean
3 egg yolks
¼ cups (2 oz./55 g)
superfine sugar

$1/3$ cup (1 ½ oz./40 g)
all-purpose flour
$5/8$ cup (150 ml) whipping
cream

FOR THE TOPPING:
¾ cup (3 ½ oz./100 g)
wild strawberries
¾ cup (3 ½ oz./100 g)
raspberries
$2/3$ cup (3 ½ oz./100 g)
blueberries
2 tablespoons toasted
sliced (flaked) almonds

Make the brioche. Preheat the oven to 325°F (165°C). In a saucepan, melt the butter and let it cool. Sift the flour and yeast into a bowl. In another saucepan, slightly warm the milk, then pour it over the flour and yeast mixture. Add the eggs and the cold melted butter. Mix to form a ball and roll this dough on a floured surface with the palm of your hand. Place the dough in a buttered terrine mold and leave it near a heat source until it has risen nearly to the top of the mold. Sprinkle the brioche with sugar. Bake it in the oven for 25 minutes, being careful that the top doesn't burn. Unmold the brioche and leave it to cool, then cut it into ¾-inch (2-cm) slices.

Prepare the brioche French toast in a bowl, beat the milk, cream, sugar, whole egg, and egg yolks. Pour this mixture into a large flat container and soak the brioche slices in it for 30 minutes, turning them several times.

Make the vanilla mousseline. In a saucepan, heat the milk with the split and scraped vanilla bean. In a bowl, whisk the egg yolks with the sugar until they turn white, then sift in the flour and combine. Pour in a ladle of hot milk to thin the mixture, then pour it into the pan. Cook without stirring for 10 minutes. Leave the crème pâtissière to cool, stirring it regularly to prevent a skin forming on top. Whip the cream until firm and fold it into the crème pâtissière. Set aside in the fridge.

Drain the slices of brioche. In a nonstick skillet, melt the butter, wait until it is beginning to foam, then add the slices of brioche. Sprinkle each slice with a pinch of brown sugar and turn over.

Place the brioche French toast on the plates and cover with the vanilla mousseline. Scatter over the red berries and the toasted almonds and serve immediately.

Enjoy with a Dom Ruinart Rosé Champagne 2006.

PROFITEROLES
WITH VANILLA CREAM AND HOT CHOCOLATE SAUCE

SERVES 6

·

PREP: 50 MINUTES
COOK: 45 MINUTES

·

Ingredients

FOR THE PROFITEROLES:
½ cup (125 ml) water
¼ cup (1 ¾ oz./50 g) butter
Pinch of salt
²/₃ cup (2 ¾ oz./75 g)
all-purpose flour
2 whole eggs
1 egg yolk

FOR CRÈME PÂTISSIÈRE:
2 cups (500 ml) milk
1 Bourbon vanilla bean
5 egg yolks
Scant ½ cup (3 ¼ oz./90 g)
superfine sugar
½ cup (2 ½ oz./70 g)
all-purpose flour

FOR THE CHOCOLATE SAUCE:
1 cup (250 ml) milk
1 cup (250 ml) whipping cream
¾ cup (3 ½ oz./100 g) grated
64% dark chocolate
1 ¾ tablespoons (1 oz./
25 g) butter
1 tablespoon peanut oil

Make the profiteroles. Preheat the oven to 350°C (170°C). In a saucepan, boil the water with the butter and salt. Add the flour all at once and mix with a spatula to thoroughly dry the dough. Remove the pan from the heat and add the two eggs, one at a time, while continuing to mix with the spatula. Carefully spoon the meringue into a piping bag fitted with a plain tip and pipe eighteen small balls on a silicone mat. Beat the egg yolk with a little water, then brush this onto the profiteroles. Dip a fork in the mixture and make a cross on each profiterole. Bake in the oven for 25 minutes.

Make the crème pâtissière. In a saucepan, heat the milk with the split and scraped vanilla bean. In a bowl, whisk the egg yolks with the sugar until they turn white, then sift in the flour and combine. Pour in a ladle of hot milk to thin the mixture, then pour it into the pan. Cook without stirring for 10 minutes. Leave the crème pâtissière to cool, stirring it regularly to prevent a skin forming on top. Set asid in the fridge.

Make the chocolate sauce. In a saucepan, boil the milk and cream. Remove from the heat and stir in the grated chocolate. Stir in the butter and peanut oil to make the sauce glossy. Keep the chocolate sauce warm in a barely hot bain-marie.

Open the profiteroles in half and fill them with the crème pâtissière. Arrange three on each dessert plate and serve with a small pot of hot chocolate sauce and, if you wish, a small dome of whipped cream.

Enjoy with a sweet Condrieu "Ayguets" 2012 by Yves Cuilleron.

RICE PUDDING
WITH SALTED BUTTER CARAMEL

Ingredients

FOR RICE PUDDING:
1 cup (7 oz./200 g) Carnaroli rice
8 cups (2 l) milk
1 Bourbon vanilla bean
5 egg yolks
¼ cup (2 ¼ oz./60 g)
superfine sugar

FOR THE CARAMEL:
½ cup (3 ½ oz./100 g)
superfine sugar
Scant ¼ cup (50 ml) water
Generous ¼ cup (1 ¾ oz./50 g)
slightly salted butter
Scant ½ cup (100 ml)
whipping cream

Make the rice pudding. In a saucepan, blanch the rice in boiling water, drain, and rinse in cold water to remove the starch. Set aside.

In a saucepan, heat the milk with the split and scraped vanilla bean. As soon as it begins to boil, add the rice and cook for 20 minutes over very low heat, stirring regularly.

Whisk the egg yolks with the sugar until the mixture becomes very frothy and creamy, then pour it, off the heat, over the cooked rice. Stir gently and set aside.

Make the caramel. In a saucepan, heat the sugar and water until caramelized and a nice amber color. Add the salted butter, cut into small pieces, and the cream. Bring it to a simmer then remove from the heat. Leave to cool.

Serve the rice pudding in pretty dishes drizzled with the salted butter caramel.

Enjoy with a Muscat "Réserve" 2016 by Trimbach.

CHOCOLATE MOUSSE
WITH A CRISPY COFFEE CONE

SERVES 6

PREP: 1 HOUR
REST: 12 HOURS
COOK: 15 MINUTES

Ingredients

FOR THE CHOCOLATE MOUSSE:
¾ cup (3 ½ oz./100 g)
grated 64% dark chocolate
½ cup espresso
5 egg whites
Pinch of salt
¼ cup (2 ¼ oz./60 g)
superfine sugar
3 egg yolks

FOR THE CONES:
$\frac{1}{3}$ cup unsifted (1 ½ oz./40 g)
confectioners' sugar
1 egg white, beaten
Generous 1/3 cup (1 ¾ oz./50 g)
all-purpose flour
4 teaspoons sunflower oil

FOR THE WHIPPED CREAM:
2 cups (500 ml) whipping cream
1 espresso

The day before, make the chocolate mousse. Melt the chocolate in a bain-marie, making sure it is no hotter than 122°F (50°C), then stir in the espresso. Whisk egg whites with the salt until just stiff. In a bowl, beat the sugar and egg yolks until the mixture turns white, then stir in the melted chocolate. Then fold in the stiffly beaten egg whites with a spatula to prevent them collapsing. Divide the chocolate mousse among six bowls and refrigerate overnight.

The next day, make the cones. Preheat the oven to 360°F (180°C). In a bowl, mix together the confectioners' sugar, beaten egg white, flour, and oil. Shape the dough into a ball, then roll it out and cut out six disks 6 inches (15 cm) in diameter. Place them on a nonstick baking sheet and bake for about 6 minutes, until nicely golden. Remove them out of the oven and immediately roll them into a cone shape. For a perfect shape, roll the still-hot discs around a metal pastry tube.

Make the whipped cream. In a large bowl, whip the cream until stiff, then slowly fold in the espresso with a spatula. Set aside in the fridge.

When the cones are completely cold, fill them with the coffee cream and serve them with the chocolate mousse.

Enjoy with a Maury "Mas Amiel Vintage" by Olivier Decelle.

PRUNES
WITH ARMAGNAC

Ingredients

7 ¾ cups (2 ¼ lb./1 kg) pitted Agen prunes
1 ½ bottles of Monbazillac
1 ½ cups (350 ml) Armagnac
1 Earl Grey tea bag
1 cinnamon stick
1 Bourbon vanilla bean

Prepare the prunes a month in advance to give them time to marinate.

Place the prunes in a jar with the Monbazillac, Armagnac, tea bag, cinnamon stick, and the vanilla bean, split in half and scraped.

Seal the jar and let the prunes marinate as long as possible (allow one month in the fridge or at least 12 days at room temperature).

Serve the prunes in bowls with their syrup and accompany them, for example, with a scoop of Berthillon Armagnac Agenaise ice cream.

Enjoy with a Graham's 15 Year Old port.

LA FONTAINE FLOATING ISLANDS

SERVES 6

·

PREP: 45 MINUTES
COOK: 40 MINUTES

·

Ingredients

FOR THE CRÈME ANGLAISE:
2 cups (500 ml) whole milk
1 Bourbon vanilla bean
5 egg yolks
⅓ cup (2 ¾ oz./80 g)
superfine sugar

FOR THE FLOATING ISLANDS:
14 oz. (400 g) egg whites
(about 12 whites)
1 ½ cups (10 ½ oz./
300 g) superfine sugar
3 ½ oz. (100 g) chopped
praline

FOR THE CARAMEL:
½ cup (3 ½ oz./100 g)
superfine sugar
4 teaspoons (20 ml) water

Make the crème anglaise. In a saucepan, heat the milk with the split and scraped vanilla bean. In a bowl, whisk the egg yolks with the sugar until they turn white. Remove the vanilla bean from the hot milk then pour it into the egg and sugar mixture and stir to combine. Pour the mixture back into the pan over medium heat, stirring continuously. To check that the crème anglaise is cooked, trace a line on the spoon: it should remain clean. Pour the crème anglaise into an ice-cold container to cool and stir regularly so that it remains smooth.

Make the floating islands. In a bowl, whisk the egg whites, starting slowly and gradually increasing the speed. Add the sugar while continuing to whisk. Set aside.

Make the caramel. In a saucepan, heat the sugar until it turns a nice amber color. Stop the cooking by adding the water, then whisk and gently heat again. Pour some of the liquid caramel into the bottom of six ramekins. Add the remaining caramel to the floating-island mixture and whisk again.

Preheat the oven to 300°F (150°C). Fill the ramekins to the brim with the floating-island mixture and sprinkle with some of the chopped praline. Add the remainder of the mixture to the ramekins, giving the floating islands a conical shape. Sprinkle with some more chopped praline. Place the ramekins in a bain-marie and bake in the oven for 15 minutes.

Leave to cool, then carefully turn them out by passing a knife around the edge of the ramekins. Wet your fingers to prevent the sugar from sticking to them and carefully place a floating island in the center of each dish. Pour the crème anglaise around the edge and serve immediately.

Enjoy with a Jurançon Petit Manseng "Clos Uroulat" 2013 by Charles Hours.

■

ACKNOWLEDGEMENTS

Thank you to our entire team at La Fontaine de Mars for their dedication and loyalty, which has helped us grow together. Without them, we could not have shaped its history over the past nearly 30 years.

Thank you to Guillaume de Laubier, without whom I would not have had the great pleasure of meeting all the wonderful "ladies" of Editions de La Martinière—remarkable women who have been kind enough to believe that our bistrot has a story to tell.

Thanks to my friend Dudu, who introduced us to photographer Delphine Constantini and her colleague, food stylist Natacha Arnoult. With relentless focus, they have revealed our everyday dishes as works of art.

Thank you to my "Godmother" aunt and to Jacques Marcassus, my friend Anne's father, the two people who, from childhood, have given me an appreciation for fine food. Without them, I would not have been able to do this job.

Thank you from the bottom of my heart to my beloved husband Jacques, for having gone along with my passionate whim to "take on" La Fountain de Mars 30 years ago. It has been him who, behind the scenes, has relentlessly organized and managed everything and has, for better or worse, allowed me to take center stage. Without him, nothing would have happened.

Christiane Boudon

Our thanks also go to:

Thierry Lemétayer, for produce from Noirmoutier and the Vendée, and Bel Espoir, for their fish;

Harry Cover, Les 4 Saisons de JR, Charraire & Primeurs Passion, and Marie Noëlle for their fruit and vegetables;

Boucherie Nivernaise, Le Coq Saint-Honore, Agriviande, Gaec Meignan, Évelyne and Franck Rozès, Pierre Oteiza, and Planquette, for their meat, poultry and offal;

Marie-Anne Cantin, La ferme d'Alexandre, and La Mère Richard, for their butter, eggs and cheeses;

Cercle Vert, for their grocery products;

Castelain and Barry, for their chocolates;

Poujauran and Laurent B, for their breads;

Laborie, Dupérier, Tradition & Gourmandises, and Chedeville, for their ducks and cured meats;

Les Belles de l'île Kalod, Les Viviers du Logeo, Viking Marée and Blanc, for their seafood;

Plantin, for their truffles.

And all the others that we've treasured for so many years.

Graphic design and production:
Laurence Maillet

Photography:
Delphine Constantini
Food styling:
Natacha Arnoult

Recipe writing:
La Fontaine de Mars
Text writing:
Cécile Maslakian

Publishing:
Virginie Mahieux assisted by **Pauline Dubuisson**

Recipe editing:
Carine Merlin
Translation from French:
Anne McDowall
Proofreading:
Mark Brutton

Abrams books are available at special discounts when purchased in quantity
for premiums and promotions as well as fundraising or educational use.
Special editions can also be created to specification. For details,
contact specialsales@abramsbooks.com or the address below.

Photoengraving: Les Caméléons
Printed and bound in December 2020 by Graphicom
ISBN: 978-1-4197-4428-0
Legal déposit: September 2019
Printed in Italy

ABRAMS
The Art of Books

195 Broadway
New York, NY 10007
abramsbooks.com